SO-FIW-568

STUDIES IN MINISTRY AND WORSHIP

EDITORS: G. W. H. LAMPE AND DAVID M. PATON

THE MISSIONARY CHURCH
IN EAST AND WEST

The Missionary Church in East and West

CHARLES C. WEST · MARLIES CREMER
T. SIHOMBING · DAVID M. PATON
A. Th. VAN LEEUWEN
J. E. LESSLIE NEWBIGIN
J. BLAUW · H.-R. WEBER

edited by
Charles C. West & David M. Paton

SCM PRESS LTD
56 BLOOMSBURY STREET
LONDON

260
W 52

FIRST PUBLISHED 1959
© SCM PRESS LTD 1959
PRINTED IN GREAT BRITAIN BY
THE CAMELOT PRESS LTD.,
LONDON AND SOUTHAMPTON

138953

CONTENTS

THIS MINISTRY:
A BIBLICAL INTRODUCTION

Charles C. West

THE subject of this book, like the meeting of pastors and missionaries at the Ecumenical Institute at Bossey from which it came, is all the more central for the fact that it lies where several boundaries meet.

For generations in many countries, the existence of missionary societies or a mission board, alongside a Church which was regarded as in its essence non-missionary, has been one of our modern anomalies. Whole theologies have been developed to justify this state of affairs. The mission has been defined as the church-planting agency, which, after bringing the seeds of the mother-church to a non-Christian land, fosters the immature sapling while it grows, until the day when a mature young Church stands on its own and the 'mission' can fade away. The Churches founded by this process have then reproduced the pattern, rejoicing in the time when their institutions become independent, their relations with other Churches 'ecumenical', and when therefore 'mission' and 'missionary' disappear.

By considering the missionary nature of the Church in the Ecumenical Institute, the writers in this book design to cut straight across this anomalous division. They aim to erase the boundary line which divides 'missions' from 'ecclesiology' and to ask the basic question, what it means to believe that the Church itself is a missionary body, at its heart and intertwined with all else that can be said to define it.

It follows from this that the chapters of this book straddle another traditional dividing line—that between home missions, or evangelism, and foreign missions. This does not mean that there is no difference between the two, or that the act of being

7

sent to the ends of the earth does not have its own meaning before God. But it has been too long assumed that home missions bear the basic character of revival, of recalling those with Christian memories, the 'lost sheep', back to the fold of the Church and the experience of salvation, while foreign missions break new ground in the pagan world. As evidence against this assumption, we present in this volume a deliberate mixture of 'foreign missionaries', 'younger churchmen' and 'home evangelists', each writing about his or her own Christian task. We believe the reader will find, as the members of the conference who first heard these talks discovered, that it is the evangelism of one Church, in what is ever more rapidly becoming one world, which is here expressed. In discovering this evangelistic task, Asians and Africans are involved with Europeans and Americans in the latter's home problems, just as surely as the reverse has been true since foreign missions began. The boundary runs not between home and foreign, between 'Christian' and 'non-Christian' lands, but between Church and world, everywhere.

This boundary between Church and world is the concern of this book. Not that it can be erased this side of the day of judgment, but that it needs to be redrawn in the light of Christ's relation to the world as it is today and of his call to the Church to evangelise such a world. This is why we present in the two following chapters radically different pictures of the world, which are rooted, not first of all in theology, but in the living experience of Christians, exercising their ministry in the world's midst. From this comes the material of theology and the source of our understanding of what it means to be the Church, and therefore a missionary Church, the instrument of God's promise and Christ's work toward the world.

It would be well to preface this, however, as was done in our Bossey conference, by considering the missionary nature of the Church as we discover it in the ministry and fellowship of the New Testament Christians themselves. We could choose illustrations from the New Testament almost at random. But the choice of Paul's words in II Corinthians, Chapters 3-6, especially the first half of Chapter 4, is nevertheless not a random one. It records Paul's pleading with the congregation at Corinth to discover the nature of its own existence as minister of the new covenant which transforms its members and reconciles the world to God. In it Paul expounds the character of the life in Christ and the direction of its apostolic character toward the world.

'Therefore, seeing we have this ministry, we faint not', reads verse I of Chapter 4. What is 'this ministry', and who are the 'we' who have been given it? There is nothing remarkable about the New Testament word 'minister' or 'ministry' in itself. In the Gospels it is used, interchangeably with the word for slavery, to indicate all kinds of service performed by one man for another, usually to his physical needs. The Old Testament word has richer overtones of personal loyalty and self-giving, but is equally common and many-sided. It is this general word which the book of Acts and the letters of Paul pick up to describe the apostolic ministry given to the whole Church first of all (Acts 1.17, 25) and in different forms to its members (I Cor. 12.5).

What the ministry here proclaimed is, is spelled out in all four of the chapters of this passage. It is the service of a new covenant (3.6), not of letters on stone, bringing judgment and death (3.7), but of the Spirit on hearts of flesh belonging to believers (3.3). As such it is a ministry of righteousness (3.9) which transforms us into the image of the glory of the Lord (3.18). In all of this it is a service done to us by God in Christ, in which we are privileged to participate and which we have therefore to make known. In making it known (4.1-3) we remain servants of all other men for Jesus' sake (4.5—the word used here is 'slaves', but the meaning is the same), ourselves only earthen vessels that the power may be of God and not of us (4.7), and living by the hope that God will raise us up (4.14 ff.). It is finally a ministry of reconciliation toward the whole world. 'God, as it were, entreating by us' (5.20) this world to accept the reconciliation which he is bringing in Christ (5.19). We are called to be servants of this great new reality, that all have died in Christ (5.14), therefore that those who live may live no longer unto themselves,

9

but unto him 'who for their sake died and was raised' (5.15).

In short, this ministry is one which is in its very nature evangelistic and missionary on the one hand, and constitutive for the Church on the other. It is the heart of what is meant by belonging to the new covenant people of God, being transformed by the Holy Spirit and living in Christ. But it is also *service* in the full sense of the word, as the Revised Standard Version translates it. It is not only communication of the Gospel by words, but the character of a communal life wherein we show that we ourselves are in fact being changed into the image of him whom we behold. Again and again in these chapters the Church is reminded that it has no being apart from that which is given it in hope as it carries about in the body the death of Jesus, so that the life of Jesus may also be manifested (4.10).

> We put no obstacle in anyone's way, so that no fault may be found with our ministry, but as servants of God we commend ourselves in every way: through great endurance, in afflictions, hardships, calamities, beatings, imprisonments, tumults, labours, watching, hunger; by purity, knowledge, forbearance, kindness, the Holy Spirit, genuine love, truthful speech and the power of God (6.3-7a).

A question, however, remains. The 'we' who have this ministry in this letter are first of all Paul himself, with his companions Timothy and Silvanus (1.19). He is commending his ministry and that of his friends to the Corinthian church, and calling that church out of its own suspicion and inner strife. He himself has been given a ministry in this case leading him to speak prophetically and pastorally to the Church. On the other hand the whole tendency of II Corinthians indicates that what Paul was claiming for himself he was claiming in principle for all Christians and for the Church as a body. His ministry to the Corinthians was an attempt to call them out to where he was, and to justify his calling as that to which all Christians are called. The apostolic ministry, the ministry of mission and evangelism, is not given directly by God to a few in the Church but to the whole Church. In the book of Acts it is only after a period of common service and common life that the ministries (6.1-6) are divided; and then by the Church for purely practical reasons.

There is, therefore, an apostolic ministry over against the Church. It may be a *charisma* which the Church, in its present forms, does not recognise or ordain. Nevertheless, this special ministry is for the Church and in the Church, a challenge to the Church to leave its false forms and ideas and become truly itself, truly apostolic and missionary over against the world in which it lives. This kind of ministry, furthermore, cannot be identified with any office or order in the Church today. It may arise anywhere, among pastors, laymen, local Christians or foreigners, or even among bishops and administrative secretaries. It is essential only that there be an inner connection between the apostle and the congregation. 'By open statement of the truth we commend ourselves to every man's conscience in the sight of God' (4.2). There is a sense in which the ministry of every apostle is validated, not by the approval of the Church, but by the Church's recognition that he is speaking to them the word of God. The same can be said of the validation of the Church's apostolic ministry by the world. One of the tragedies of our time is that the Church's failure to find itself in this ministry has led to distorted forms of prophecy in movements such as Communism and nationalistic reactions to imperialism.

This leads to the second large question which this passage raises—that of the solidarity of the Church with the world to which it ministers. No place in the Bible is sharper in drawing the issue: 'If our Gospel is veiled, it is veiled only to those who are perishing. In their case the god of this world has blinded the minds of the unbelievers, to keep them from seeing the light of the Gospel of the glory of Christ, who is the likeness of God' (4.3-4). Who are the perishing? One could interpret the word to apply only to those who have had the Gospel presented to them and have somewhat wilfully rejected it. Paul seems especially to have had in mind the Judaisers on the one hand and the Gnostics on the other (Chs. 11-12). In our day this might mean those who are involved in religious or ideological reactions against the Christian faith—Communist, nationalist, Muslim, Hindu, Buddhist. And when we think this way we must remember that attempts to build up the Christian religion in western lands as a bulwark of our own cultural pride or peace of mind fall under the same condemnation. But the group which studied this passage at Bossey came to the unanimous conclusion that all of us, Church and world alike, stand under the judgment of this verse. There are two forms in which the perishable nature of our life is presented to us in these chapters: that of the veil which obscures the Gospel (3.13-16; 4.3), and that of the earthen vessel which contains it (4.7). Both perish. We are all therefore tempted, by the fact that we are mortal, self-interested and sinful, to construct such a religion, even with Christian dogmas, as veils the Gospel. This, as Paul points out (Ch. 3), is what the Jews did with the Law, which, it seems clear, was not intended as a 'ministry of death' at all, but as guidance unto life. It is this which makes us preach ourselves, and not Christ Jesus the Lord and ourselves as servants for his sake (4.5). On the other hand, those for whom the Gospel is not veiled are those who have learned what it means to be overcome by the grace of God in Christ, and so to act as earthen vessels which rejoice in their own destruction at the proper time in order that the life of Jesus may be manifested (4.7-12). This means, practically, a solidarity with those who are perishing which takes every form of pride and superiority out of our message. The Church has nothing in this world to defend; it has the whole power of Christ in every part of the world to manifest.

> We are treated as impostors, and yet are true; as unknown, and yet well known; as dying, and behold we live; as punished, and yet not killed; as sorrowful, yet always rejoicing; as poor, yet making many rich; as having nothing, and yet possessing all things (6.8b-10).

This immediately raises the question about those churches which are in fact anything but the modest earthen vessels whose life and witness these words describe. What of the prosperous church? What of the 'National Church' in a Christian country?

What of the Christian life where there has been no suffering? To raise these questions is to apply the central message of this passage about the missionary nature of the Church to the reform and renewal of our churches, missions, schools, hospitals, and prosperous lives, in order that they may become vehicles for the life of Jesus, by sharing in faith the perishability of all things in this world, in his death.

To this renewal and this apostolate there is an eschatological urgency. The Greek of Chapter 4 verse 6 puts it plainly: 'It is God who said, "Light shall shine out of darkness," who shined in our hearts for the sake of the knowledge of the glory of God in the face of Jesus Christ.' God has shined in our hearts in order that his glory might be known in the world. The Church is therefore in motion toward the world just insofar as it receives this glory with unveiled face, and accepts the death and transformation it brings with it.

What then is this world which confronts us today when we look at it in the perspective of Christ's work toward it? What form would a church take which would be capable of bearing witness to the death and transformation which is the substance of missionary presence in that world? To these questions the remaining chapters of this book are devoted.

THE CHURCH IN THE WORLD: THE BROKEN WEST

Marlies Cremer

A PRELIMINARY word: I must request the reader himself to form an objective picture of what I have to say. I must speak from a subjective standpoint since I did not experience National Socialism in Germany from outside but from within. I would also add that I do not speak as a theologian but as a social scientist.

What is the Church's service to those outside its life in Germany today? In the first place it is a service among those already baptized. More than 90 per cent of all Germans are baptized, nominal Christians, who often regard the Church as an institution for the conduct of ceremonies. I can illustrate this with an experience of my own. A man came into the church office to order a funeral. I told him that a representative of the pastor would have to conduct it because the pastor himself was otherwise occupied. When the man saw this representative—a small, unimposing dɜɹson, barely five feet tall—he refused, and demanded the venerable pastor, with his white hair. After all, he could not do that to his grandmother: have her buried by a little man, barely five feet tall!

Therefore the least part of the Church's service is among its voluntary members, since only about 6 per cent of the baptized come to church services and far less to other church meetings as well. Pastors and parish workers must seek out other opportunites —in industry, for example, or, as part of their training, by attending trade union courses—where people cannot evade them. Their presence there may lead to a request for a church service and to discussion on questions of daily life: marriage, family, politics, to all of which the Christian must have something to say. Or we ourselves, as the Church, can hold meetings to a certain extent in competition with secular institutions, perhaps for vocational groups. The industries recognise our conferences and give their workers paid leave to attend them, as they do for the trade unions and other groups. Other social work is done in co-operation with secular institutions. Young people especially take part in these courses because the questions discussed are relevant to their personal lives, and not primarily because they want to hear the message of Jesus Christ.

Who are the people who do this kind of work? In the first place they must be people with special training. We have many pastors who are specialists on such questions as pensions, piece work, or wage policy. But pastors cannot do the whole of this work. Mature members of the congregation can also help, provided they have some expert knowledge. We expect a leading social worker in the Church to have, as well as his spiritual qualities, some professional qualification which gives him authority. Our colleagues in this work are men who can express themselves so effectively, even in a trade union meeting where they are not known, that they are nominated and often even elected as delegates. Thus, well-known men in the social work of the Evangelical Churches have rejected many posts in which the world has sought their services, while some have felt called as Christians to accept such secular positions. In all events these men must have such high qualifications because our work is a service of the congregation *in the world*.

It was a good deal easier for the apostles to reach their fellow-men. They had the synagogue or the market place, where men gathered. But we have no common meeting-place in our world, either in the sense of location, or in our habits and in our thinking.

Nor do we have a time when all men can come together. The time of Sunday services or other meetings is no longer possible for many men and almost never for the shift worker. We have a strange new relationship to time which we have not clarified at all. We live in different rhythms of life. The life rhythm which we church workers have—forced to do intellectual work in the evening—does not suit many workers. They simply cannot think after a day of hard physical labour, especially the women. They have a completely different rhythm of life from ours. There is hardly a place in the world where we are all present in the same way, even if we are present together in body. Some are there expecting to work with their minds; others are so tired that they cannot do this, and need some form of relaxation.

Finally, there is no trust in our society. There is no place where every man can say, 'This is where I can come and belong.' He leaves his home and environment only to pursue his own interests. He goes, for example, to an Evangelical Academy meeting, where he will not be committed to anything, rather than to a congregation.

The situation which I have sharply sketched here is a situation following upon a complete spiritual and moral collapse. This collapse did not begin in 1945, or in 1933. Its roots lie much further back: first of all, in the general social development by which the place of living and the place of work become separated. Earlier man lived and worked completely within the family, which was the centre of cultural and social life. Now these aspects of living have become separated from one another. Society is something like an ellipse whose two centres are work and family. In between is empty space. But with this separation of life from work there also came, in the West, the replacement of an old order by a new one, whose beginnings lie in the French Revolution, with its proclamation of Liberty, Equality and Fraternity. In Germany, living under a patriarchal hierarchy, problems of equality remained long unsolved. There every quest, whether implicit or explicit, for these new democratic forms failed, with the result that public life in Germany had no unified structure and there was no general democratic consciousness as in England. Rather, our history was one of uncompleted revolutions. Because we had no common democratic foundation we concentrated on work and the family.

This was our social situation before National Socialism. There was no truly common spiritual orientation. Different forms of life and order ran alongside one another, with the relations between them completely unclear. The democratic beginnings of 1919 had not yet ripened.

But how was it with the Church? Did we have a common foundation there? As a result of the Enlightenment the most important elements in the Evangelical Church were either lost or weakened: the Word as event, the Word in its helping power, the Word of blessing, of forgiveness in repentance and in the Sacrament. The Word became human talk. Important traditions were thereby already called in question, paving the way for the Liberalism which came later. The Evangelical Church remained as it had been since Luther: bound to the local nobility. The lord of the village or district was at the same time the head of the church. The last German Kaiser, for example, had the right to preach, even in exile. And therefore the nobility interfered with the liturgy and the church constitution. This feudal order conditioned in many cases the forms of life. This was the situation at the beginning of the Nazi period: no common social foundation, a weakened Church, and many unclarified questions.

At this point I must become personal. I was then a young woman looking for solutions to the problems which pressed on all of us young people at that time. I come from a pastor's family, but was educated as a Liberal. My father was not active in the ministry because he could not reconcile it with his Liberal convictions. Against this background we faced the social question: what is our attitude to the worker? and the national question: what is Germany's place in Europe? Behind us was a war which we had lost. I remember well how we had to ride through the 'Polish Corridor' to reach East Prussia. What kind of an order is it, when one must travel through a foreign country to come into one's own? What holds us together? What is our common basis?

I began to study in 1932 and was at first completely engrossed in it. Then came National Socialism, which spread through the country like an awakening. The word 'Socialism' sank deep into our hearts as young students. In Freiburg we said to one another: 'We can never make a revolution by studying.' They called us from outside to come and help, which meant that we left the university and went into labour service. We had lost enough time in discussion. We had worn out our minds on questions which we still did not understand, without ever getting our hands dirty. Now was the time to stand alongside the working man. So we went to East Prussia, where there was great need, and tried to help the farmers and to relieve our bad consciences. We worked together under the most primitive conditions and our life was 'a romantic experience'. This was our experience of National Socialism. Life, the earth that we held in our hands, everything, was romantic: to live in primitive labour camps, to work with the farmers and to make ourselves take orders from these men who were culturally inferior to us—all this was romantic. We believed that we were experiencing true fraternity, and we saw how thankful they were. This led me through social service to National Socialism, because I believed there was no other way. I had no theological foundation to guide me.

We tried to make National Socialism our philosophy of life. The Nazis emphasised propaganda among students because they believed they represented Germany's future. 'You know that all revolutions are uncompleted, but we will complete them.' 'We shall solve the problem which the Socialists sought to solve: the true place of the worker. But we will not separate the worker from the people. We are not international socialists. We will solve the social problem within our people.' Such ideas as these had a tremendous power to mislead young people who still had no spiritual foundation. We did not recognise the primitive nature of this force which was hypnotising us. We believed we were making a great sacrifice when we moved into a human society which was not only crude, but irrational and unpleasant in its expression. When we are asked today whether we did not feel ourselves repelled for aesthetic reasons by the lack of culture and taste which we met, I can only answer yes. But we believed that we must make this sacrifice. We owed it to true fraternity. Thus one young generation looked at National Socialism. Those younger than we were still less critical, for they knew still less of another world than we. We believed that this was the hour of spiritual meaning.

A Christian could clearly see where it would lead, but we could not. I was only amazed, but not disgusted, by its tendencies. Let

me give you an example. At a memorial ceremony for the war dead
in Berlin, a professor of political science said in his speech—I
almost hesitate to repeat his blasphemy—'Adolf Hitler has overcome death in victory'. He wanted to make clear to us that the
dead of the first world war had not perished in vain. Adolf Hitler
would make their death fruitful. Their death meant our duty to
fight for a new Germany. That such things could be said to us at
all showed that everything in our world was completely distorted.

When we read *Faust* we saw his longing fulfilled here: 'to stand
on free land with a free people'. Events of German history, dismissed too quickly before, were now discussed at great length—
Romanticism was rediscovered—and all this reached its culmina-
tion in Adolf Hitler. You can understand that men who suddenly
believed that they stood in a unique historical hour were prepared
to make sacrifices *en masse* as they never had before. 'If we make
sacrifices now, then everything which has happened till now in
Germany, all the failures and lost opportunities, can be made
good.' This was the mood not only among students but also workers, and especially among people who had lost relatives during
the first world war. 'If you are loyal, then your fathers, your
husbands and your sons will live on. They will live on if you give
all your strength in the service of National Socialism.' This appeal
made men demand sacrifices of themselves and perform tasks
of which they never would have thought themselves capable.
When you see the experience in this light you can understand
how much National Socialism absorbed and assimilated into
itself, chosen as it was, voluntarily, by a large section of the people.
Its view of the past fascinated us again and again. It hid from us
the fact that National Socialism had no real programme for the
future and no real solution to our problems. Its outlook on the
future was thoroughly romantic. For the farmer it spoke of 'blood
and soil'. We dressed ourselves again in peasant costume, learned
home weaving, revived ancient customs and other romantic
luxuries which in the long run could not be borne by the German
economy. For the common life of industry National Socialism
offered a solution which came out of a completely different social

order: that of the leader and his yeoman, an utterly impossible concept for present day industry. The Nazis simply ignored the unavoidable tensions between employer and employees, the questions of property, and all the real problems we faced. But they did so with great skill and spirit, and we young people allowed ourselves to be drawn into the romance.

But where did the Church stand in relation to all this? The Church as a whole was not interested in social questions, and those pastors who were concerned about them in many cases tended in the earliest period, even before 1933, to support National Socialism. It is clear that at this point something was lacking in the Church. A number of church youth groups stood in danger of being carried off by Nazism simply because the continuing social problems of Germany were more pressing for them than for the Church as a whole. It was for these young people a spiritual revolution when after two or three years they withdrew from Nazism again, many at great personal cost because they had to give an official explanation for their withdrawal.

Was anything happening then in the Church? It was intensively occupied with theological renewal, at first purely on an intellectual level. But then, by the miracle of God's grace, this intellectual theology became the tool of the Church in action. The theologians gave the Church a weapon against National Socialism, the armour it needed to be the watchman of the social conscience. Everything depended on this office of watchman and prophet. A clear line had to be drawn between Church and State based on biblical theology itself: Romans 13; Revelation 13; and the Prophets. Bible study took on a new importance, for example on the Prophet Amos. I still remember how in Nazi circles we scornfully thought: 'All they can do in the Church is to dig out an old prophet, and a minor prophet at that!' Yet Amos was a decisive figure for the Church in those days. He led to something still more important: a political confession of the Church toward the world. The circles which gathered around Dietrich Bonhoeffer and others found in the office of the prophetic watchman an obligation toward the world which they expressed in worldly terms. This was Bonhoeffer's great and decisive act. He was condemned by the Nazis, not only because he had worked with 'churchly' means but because he had also undertaken to go in the midst of the world with a conscience bound to Christ. With the men of July 20th, 1944[1] he worked with the means of this world, in this world.

Then a third thing happened: the Church found a new and living form. It seemed ridiculous from outside. It is hard to imagine today with what scornful certainty Nazi circles made fun of it. Yet the Church rediscovered itself. Congregations were formed in concentration camps, barracks and prisons. Christians met always under difficulties because it was forbidden to gather openly. They stood together on stairways or met with apparent casualness in some neutral place. They met in bomb-shelters, waiting for the bombs, and bore their witness there. This was the congregation, a congregation which had power. It was open to Communists and Jews. Jews were hidden in Christian houses without questions about a different faith, race, or *weltanschauung*.

In this process something else became clear: in some situations Christians act in exactly the same way as mature men who know nothing of Christ. It was a great challenge to the Church that Christians could meet with others, even with Communists, and do something together without having a common faith. It placed before the Church the question of its action in the world.

Thus the Church grew in the midst of this social disintegration. Church buildings were destroyed by bombs, but this only helped the Church to become in the truest sense of the words a 'pilgrim people', a 'people on the way' towards God's promise.

And then came the collapse. Suddenly, the suffering Church became a triumphant Church. Everything else was shattered and destroyed. Only the Church was left. And the people came to it not for the sake of its message but simply because it was the one remaining reality. It was there wherever it was needed. It buried the dead, took care of the sick, mediated between quarrellers.

[1] The 20th July, 1944, was the date of an attempt on Hitler's life combined with a plot to take over the German government led by a number of leading figures in political and military circles, with the support also of many churchmen.

Pastors were ready to do everything necessary, wherever people were in need, and all was done in God's service.

But then the picture changed: the Church began to invite people both literally and figuratively into the ruins. It began to build up the old churches as they had been before; to buy bells— bells which *had* to be bigger than those in the neighbouring church —while it had no money to build club rooms for youth. The new theology remained: it had proved itself. The office of prophetic watchman continued to be exercised and preached. Yet for us in youth work this often becomes a great difficulty in practice, be- cause the wholeness of the Church's service to society tends now to be forgotten in the interest of this one aspect. I realise what the new theology has meant and what it still means for us; but the strong dominance of theologians with this single line of approach to the world has become a problem for our Church today.

Let me return to society and myself after the Nazi collapse. I was quite strange to the Church. In all the last days I often asked where all this was leading. But it was the question of a Roman Catholic which first gave me a sense of direction, when he asked, in the middle of a market place: 'What does it mean for you to be human?' This question haunted me; I was shocked to find that I had no answer to it. I thought back to the crudity of much that we had thought and done in the Nazi time. Where in fact was our concern for the human? We did many things, all with a certain confusion, in the illusion that everything was being done for Man. What was humanity? Then came the collapse, and with it the annihilation of everything we had built up. It is hard for anyone outside this experience to realise what it meant. I knew that all my professional training, everything which I had learned, was now useless. All my education had been held together as it were by a magnet; and now that this magnet was gone what I had learned was nothing but dust and débris. Many of us were in this state. Not only was everything we had owned destroyed but also everything we had believed in. It was only by God's grace that we survived. For years we were neither able, nor allowed, to teach history in our schools, except the ancient history of Greece, which

I taught! We had no common past and looked to no common future. Some of us had sat in concentration camps during the Third Reich and some of us afterwards. We did not know what would become of us. Even suffering, which usually brings men together, divided us. We acknowledge no common guilt. We all pushed our guilt into the past or on to others instead of recognising that we shared it. Even today the question of national guilt threatens our whole community. When a politician of the older generation rises to the top he will be certain to buy *Der Spiegel* every week. *Der Spiegel* is a German political magazine which delights in stirring up mud from the past; and there is no one who is so free of guilt that he can be confident of being left out.

This question of guilt even penetrates church circles and places before us the serious question: how are we to bind up the wounds and to bridge the divisions of our past? That it is possible to do so is proved perhaps by my presence with you here today. The person who was invited to speak and who asked me to replace him suffered under National Socialism on the other side from me. Yet we believe, as members of the same congregation, that each of us will express what is important for the other. This work of reconciliation, of making real the forgiveness which Christ offers and the new beginning in him, is a healing work of the Church in our society which is far from complete. How often have I been asked during my many journeys around Germany: 'Please give so-and-so my very special greetings; and please don't forget. He stood in those days on the other side and does not dare to take the first step towards friendship again.' Most of us still stand alone: only in exceptional cases have we found community again.

Behind the German 'economic miracle' is a terrible spirit of private competition. Each of us uses all available resources to outdo the other. Formerly workers in a factory were bound to one another by their common task. They found in it personal satisfaction and responsibility, and the way to further influence. But today we have made the factory into a completely private affair, where each man works for his own advancement. He would like to live as well as he did before or perhaps better, and the factory is a means to this end and nothing more. When a man has built up his private business or profession or earns a good salary, then he is 'somebody' again. Once again he commands the respect of others, which he may have lost through his Nazi activities or the weakness resulting from war or imprisonment, and with the respect of his family and society he regains his self-respect.

Even the family has become an institution which one uses to find security. In the earlier post-war days the family shared its income in order to establish itself as a group. But now the family lives for itself and not even with the neighbourhood. It is the stepping stone to position and power. Outside the family groups are not formed for common service but only for special interests through which people hope to broaden their horizon and thereby cope with a larger part of this world. So they advance, step by step privately. There may be some unity against Communism. People do not want to be deceived again. Communism would only succeed in West Germany if it were able to prove that it could raise the West German standard of living and yet leave the people to go on living their private lives in their own way.

This is how our present day society lives, split into small interest groups, isolated from one another. The person who lives in this isolated private realm is fully enclosed in the laws of the world. He has mastered them somewhat; he knows what he must do to get ahead. He does not expect too much and tries to get around the world by its own laws. It is not surprising that modern man often says that he can get along without God. When we look at it realistically, he lives a remarkably one-sided existence: a purely wordly one.

Modern man has a distinctive, new relation to time. For example, when we work at the assembly line in a factory we are only present with half our being. When someone addresses us there we cannot answer with our whole personality because we do not have strength or concentration for anything other than the work which we are doing, even though this work does not engage our whole personality. We have, so to speak, no full existence there. The same situation, which only allows us to be half alive or superficially present during our work, meets us again at home in front of the television: the picture is there on the screen, but the human being—our neighbour—is missing. We have almost got used to half existing everywhere, and the result is a hectic running after experiences because we feel that something is missing. And yet all of our many experiences do not bring us a full existence. We believe that real existence is something we must seek. We try to balance our partial lives. Yet we find only another part, because we are seeking new stimuli instead of a genuinely new life.

This is not a problem of morals. It is the modern world of work itself which puts the problem to us and shows us that we have not solved it. There are jobs where the sharpest kind of attention and strong nervous tension is a simple necessity, but where there is practically no movement of the body. What real compensation can such workers receive? And how can their social powers be freely exercised? Are we really free in our 'free time' after work? Can we use its opportunities? Or do we not find the quick change from high tension work to complete freedom, from working day to evening rest, from week-day to week-end, from job to vacation, beyond our powers?

The final result for many is simply resignation. I often find among young people with whom I have to do the following attitude: 'Friendship?—No, I do not go in for that any more. I would rather not be disappointed.' Every man cuts himself off from other men and faces alone the task of orientating himself in a broken world. Men seek a new relation to space and time but have given up the attempt to form their common life anew. The problem of their 'partial presence', their half-existence, hinders this. They seek to orientate themselves anew in a world whose forms have all changed. The social scientist knows that a genuine new orientation must go together with new creativity, and this is never possible for the individual, but only through human co-operation. This is a fact of social science. But it is precisely this which is so terribly difficult today because society is composed of little groups, fortified and isolated over against each other: they no longer expect anything of co-operation on a larger scale. They prefer to forget the problem of their relation to other men, which after all they cannot control. Many seek help from psychology but use it far too often only to defend themselves against others. To learn to know another person and his reactions is to be able to calculate what he will do, so that there is no longer need to fear him: he is in one's power. One does not dare, however, to open oneself to him or to come out of one's own isolation into the community. One remains alone even though one deals with others.

What position does the Church take in all this?

The Church also shares this condition. Its traditions have been virtually shattered. They are no longer applicable as they are, although we seem unable to make this fact apparent. The Church is just as split and torn as society. In a few places, to be sure, it tries to bind up and heal society's wounds, where Christians hold influential positions. There are two approaches here. There are men who understand the task God has given them as a service and not as the exercise of power; and there are others who declare: 'We must have authority again'. For us social workers this word 'again' is painful, because it seeks to take us back to what has been. But there is no future for us there. We must find new forms which are really helpful for our time. We must recognise as Christians that we do not yet have them. What do we have? Our theology has been given. It helps us to be alert in East and West. The Church is still today in a position to say a helpful 'no' to society. We have good preachers who still know how to speak this judgment. But we find it much more difficult to say the proper 'yes': the yes which opens the way to new social formation. We are faced furthermore with the fact that many people are no longer open to verbal preaching of any kind. During the Nazi period we had speakers who could carry masses with them. Even the power of the word was perverted in those days. Today this distrust of words turns itself against the word of the Church. National Socialism pulled the word of the Church with it down into its collapse.

The Church, we must admit, is quite as helpless as the world when it comes to finding new forms of common life. In our Provincial Churches, Free Churches, and others, we attempt again and again to come together in the most varied kinds of organisation and we discover that the Spirit is at work in them. But a new form of Church God has not given us. The Church exists today—it cannot do otherwise—in these acts of service.

In the last century *diakonia* meant service of the individual. Today it means service of the whole society. Believing ourselves to have been sent, we join political groups, simply to be present there. We carry our message, our intercession and our help to people in the places where they are. We realise that in so doing we ourselves are in danger of giving in to the world where we should not. But we must conform to the world: Jesus Christ did, in a certain way at least. We often fall into temptation, but there is a greater temptation for the Church: to withdraw in pride. We know that whether we are in the traditional Church or in new branches of Christian work, we need one another's help and correction. We even have money, as the world—at least in Germany—has money. With it we can build homes and institutions, academies, hospitals, schools, and the rest. But can we live in these institutions in a common spirit? There are so many tensions in the German Church that we approach each synod-meeting with anxious expectation, because it brings with it the danger that there may be a split in the Church. For the newspapers this is a scandal. But, surprisingly enough, people who are quite outside the Church do not find it so. They see these tensions rather as a sign of the seriousness with which the Church takes its task. They see a certain openness to the world in the fact that the Church allows itself to be questioned and criticised from within. They may even be led to a new kind of confidence in us. A world which is isolated in itself will not come to us for the sake of the Gospel, but only to raise the vital issues in its own life. The world dares to come to the Church only where it knows that it will find not ready-made answers but a willingness to struggle with unsolved problems.

We who have been placed in the midst of all these tensions discover unexpectedly that we can help the world through the solidarity of common questioning. When a man begins to ask questions he takes thereby the first step away from the superficiality of his existence. Is it not our task as a Christian congregation, in a world which no longer dares to ask questions, to make men free by our very existence alongside them and to express the questions which are in their hearts ? This is not a question of method, but of whether the Christian congregation is prepared to live in openness both to God and the neighbour, whether it is prepared to die with Christ, whether it is prepared to offer to him without reserve its entire organisation and existence in order that he may tear it down and build it anew. The central question for us is whether we are in the midst of the world as men who pray, as a congregation of Christ, even when we cannot preach the Word. We do not know whether there will be an opportunity to speak the word of God or when it will come, but we pray that God will give to the Christian congregation a total existence before him in the world. The men of this world suffer, in the last analysis, because they are enclosed in its laws, its calculations and its struggles for power. The congregation of Christ stands in the midst of this world and shares its suffering in every way. But through the questioning and self-questioning of this congregation God enables it to bear witness to the grace of Jesus Christ, which makes us free.

THE CHURCH IN THE WORLD:
AN ASIAN VIEW

T. Sihombing

IN this subject we are dealing with a question which is central to our thinking as Christians; so central that there is a great tradition of thinking about it which has run through the international church conferences of the last thirty years: Tambaram, Whitby, Lund, Willingen and Evanston, all have made their contribution. One might well ask what justification there is for an Asian churchman to take the matter up afresh. The answer, I believe, lies in the fact that these great conferences have been interrupted in their thinking by a great world war, by revolutions, and by the rise of new nations. The problem we face is an old one, but the situation in which we face it is continually changing. It is therefore wise to re-examine our common thinking in the Ecumenical Movement ever afresh, if we are to see clearly in each new situation what our mission is.

Let me first set the scene of the Asian society as it was and as it has become under the influence of the West.

The static traditional agrarian life of Asia differs greatly from the dynamic and productive forces of European society. Economic conditions have been almost unchanged from century to century; people have worked patiently in rice fields and have produced just sufficient corn and maize for their needs. Sometimes a dry season caused great danger of starvation. Heads of villages could not increase the prosperity of the villagers because of the poor methods of production. At the same time the difference between poor and rich was very great. Princes lived in magnificent palaces which resembled small towns, built by the cheap labour of the people. They heaped up riches drawn from the people. They enjoyed power and prosperity while the common people had no share in power. Their sweat and blood was shed for this small upper ruling class. So beside the wealthy we found the indescribable grinding poverty of the working people in Asia. Into this situation of stable subsistence agriculture and great contrasts between rich and poor, ruler and ruled, the power of western imperialism and capitalism has come.

Politically speaking, the East knows the West as it has entered his home, as an uninvited guest. It judges the West by its behaviour. The Asian knows nothing of the fact that western man also has his own home. He does not know how the western man behaves in his home when he is surrounded by his children, his books and flowers. The oriental knows the westerner as the unwelcome foreigner, who is impatient, domineering, fearsome, and who is so different from him in appearance and behaviour. European powers conquered several strongholds of Asia and proceeded to dispute for control of the larger oriental states. But in doing so they soon adapted themselves to oriental patterns of ruling. As a rule the westerners dealt only with the oriental princes and feudal chiefs and they succeeded in obtaining a part of the inter-Asian traffic in fine quality products, the object of oriental trade for centuries.

In the economic field western impact made itself felt in various ways, according to the political relationships between the western power and the eastern society. The growth of British industry served to bring about a fundamental change in relationships between East and West. The expanding textile industry in England was in constant need of a regular supply of our materials. Conversely, the products of European industry were in search of a market in the East.

So the bases of eastern society were shaken for the first time by western capitalism. On the whole, however, the same general development could be observed in the various Asian countries, although there was a time lag between similar processes in different countries. Indian society was the first to feel the effects of western capitalism. British colonial power succeeded in forcing British products on Indian society, and the railways she built across India made it possible for British goods to be delivered. In China the impact of British textiles served to disrupt the closed economy of the Chinese village, for the farmer was now in need of money in order to pay for the clothes which had before been homespun. In most parts of Java home industry also gradually gave way to the import of cotton prints, first from England, later chiefly from Holland. The introduction of a money economy into Asian countries was the first effect of western capitalism. The farmer was no longer able to base his production almost exclusively on home consumption; he had to look for a supplementary money income. As a result, he was involved in production for the world market and became dependent on price fluctuations. Some peasants became growers of market crops. Others had to provide for a supplementary income as labourers on commercial crop plantations. Both these new kinds of work were disruptive of Asian village life. Many traditional institutions were gradually forced to give way. Family property, not transferable before, was transformed into individual property which could be mortgaged for debt. Among ordinary villagers there were some who attained prosperity under the new system and therefore challenged the privileges of the hereditary chiefs. On the other hand the majority of the peasants ran into debt because more or less proletarianised. Of course, these people resented the new state of things; they lost the sense of security that tradition and membership of a collective group had given them. Agrarian society was being atomised and the peasant felt isolated and frustrated by forces that he could not master or even understand. As a result, peasant uprisings became a general characteristic of the Asian countries. In their traditional way these uprisings aimed at the overthrow of the dynasties that had failed in averting distress from the peasantry. But after a short hesitation the western powers chose the policy of backing the oriental imperial and feudal rulers and by doing so propped up the collapsing feudal structure.

The most striking social phenomenon in Asia was the enormous prestige of the white race as a consequence of its military and political domination. The new social state of affairs was most manifest in Java-Indonesia. The Javanese ruling class was kept in its superior position over the native population, and the colonial power made use of the traditional oriental structure in order to strengthen its hold on the people. Even so the native ruling class was forced to adapt itself to western governmental practices and to lend support to western capitalist forces. The legal authority of this class was given the backing of colonial power; but at the same time it lost something of its traditional patterns. Moreover, the high social prestige of western ways caused the ruling class to adopt some of them; thus a smaller upper layer of Indonesians tried to conform to western standards of living and thinking. One of the Indonesian leaders, Sutan Sjahrir, said in one of his books:

> Am I now a stranger amidst my own people? Why do I say that the old patterns have no meaning or value to me? According to culture I am closer to America or Europe than to the Islamic culture of Sumatra or Java. What is our basis? Is it Europe or is it the ruins of the feudalistic culture which we can still find in our people?

That is the tragedy we now feel in Asia.

In the other most important Asian countries the situation was somewhat different. In India a white ruling class had made a place for itself at the top of the social pyramid as a sort of super-caste. But the number of colonial Britishers in India remained very restricted. A more or less westernised Indian bourgeoisie consisting of industrialists, merchants and intellectuals arose in the wake of westerners. In China the white man was apparently never able to attain a position comparable to that in colonial countries. But the difference was more one of degree than one of kind. After the opium war, by means of military expeditions and treaties the whites gradually achieved a special status.

In colonial countries western education gave an oriental the ability to fill leading posts in government and private enterprise from which the system imposed by the West on its colonies had excluded him. Therefore those who stood nearest to western culture often became the fiercest adversaries of western representatives in the East. Western education had the effect of dynamite upon the colonial status system, and so for the first time there was introduced a dynamic factor with sufficient force to revolutionise the total structure of eastern society. The peoples of Asia had yet to find an equally dynamic response to this stimulus introduced from without.

Asia of today is quite different from Asia of four centuries ago. Whereas at that time contemplation and static religion was the highest good of every man, now we find dynamic resources. Asia cries out for freedom and justice and for the prosperity which it believes will be the outcome of freedom and justice, though it has much to go through before it succeeds in abandoning old structures and old ways of living. Asia protests against backwardness in politics and technical skills. Modernisation is being led by the Asian governments and backed by the peoples' movements. The growth of nationalism, whether moderate or extreme, is one answer of the whole of Asia to colonialism and imperialism. The Asian nations demand full responsibility in administering their own business and in determining their own position in international affairs. They want to be recognised as equals by other nations, no longer subject to western rulers. While the second world war occupied the West opportunity came to the East to break free from western imperialism.

The astonishing development of education, modern farming, the abolition of feudalism, the change in women's rights, are factors in the changing situation which prove attractive to the people. Communist propaganda in such a situation appeals to Asians. It gives them hope and messianic promise in their poverty. Atheism and materialism are challenges to the truth of the Gospel and they also result in the devaluation of the old eastern religions. It must also be mentioned that the problem of the totalitarian character of Communism is not relevant because the people have never lived under a real democracy. Communist influence is active, secretly and publicly. The recent general elections in Indonesia show us that the Communist party gets most of the votes in the poor areas, in the slums and in the plantations. It is also true that what happens in Russia creates a deep impression on the non-Communist leaders in Asia. They are closer to the West than to

Russia in their political conceptions, but they see clearly that the Russian revolution provides power for national activities. Another influence, socialism, is also trying to improve the conditions of the working class in a more parliamentary way and is also opposing imperialism. So we see that nationalism, Communism and socialism are working side by side in one front against colonialism. Everywhere there is unrest, rebellion, corruption and political assassination.

But on the other hand we have also made several positive achievements. Constitutional freedom gives a chance to a great number of Asian people to train themselves in the field of government administration. The Labour parties get a chance. The feeling of political responsibility becomes more intense with the growth of the political parties. Native traders, supported by the government, are better enabled to make improvements in the field of economy and technique. Education spreads its wings widely in various countries in Asia, which would have been impossible under colonial governments. Thirst for knowledge is very apparent in Asia, and national culture is born. Youth movements help to make young people more conscious of responsibility towards the welfare of their countries. Various gigantic problems have yet to be solved in Asia; starvation, high mortality rate, limited education, even the lack of simple machinery; but efforts for improvement should come from the Asian people themselves. Asia has found energy and power within herself whereby to carry out her huge duty.

What then is the message of the Church against this background? It rests fundamentally not on our action but on the work of God in Jesus Christ. Three decisive moments may be discerned in the action of Jesus in constituting the *ecclesia*. First, he called disciples and taught them. Second, he sent them forth to proclaim the Gospel both by word and deed. Third, at the Last Supper he instituted a new covenant with them and called them as a new people of God. From the beginning of biblical history it was the congregation, rather than individuals, which was the object of God's call. But this new people of God was distinguished from the old by its dedication to a mission on behalf of the whole world, to proclaim the coming of the kingdom of God. By the kingdom Jesus means neither earthly utopia nor heavenly paradise, but rather God's kingly rule as an ever-present fact, always seeking entry into human life. It has come among men with the coming of Christ himself. The kingdom is therefore at hand in Jesus' preaching, teaching and healing, and men are called to enter in. Mark 3.13-19 was the setting apart of a Christian group for the apostolic work of evangelism. The apostles were sent on a special mission. They were given authority and power. They were made witnesses to the things they had seen and heard and taken part in. The Church is the messianic community living between the time of the manifestation of the Messiah and the fulfilment of his kingdom. So the Church has always a missionary task to fulfil and always lives amid the tension of the actual temporal order and the divine eternal order. The Church is the community constituted by faith in Jesus Christ as Lord and Saviour. The Church as the Body of Christ, sharing his life, has a ministerial function derived from that of Christ. In this function every member has his place and share according to his different capabilities and calling. Jesus, while on earth, intended that there should be this continuing Church and this continuing ministry of himself and his servants. Nevertheless we must seek to emphasise what Christ emphasised, and if we were to pick one thing as being supremely important, it would be that Christ insisted that the ministry is apostolic in a missionary sense. The task given to the apostles was the upbuilding of the Church and the extension of the kingdom, and they are *servants* of the Church. They are not a special class of men who have had delegated to them the right of excusing people from punishment by absolving them from sin. They share in the life of the Risen Lord to such an extent that they can do what he did. They continue the ministry of the Lord. Thus they represent the Church. In this they can rely on his presence and the power of the Spirit. This evangelism is not a man's own enterprise, not the Church's own enterprise: it is the overflowing of the love of Christ into the world. Our message is to the people now living. It is to invite them to that decision of faith in him by which they are made sharers in the eternal world. The very character of the Church's deeds of love and service is surely determined by this reference to the eternal kingdom. The citizens of heaven are to carry out the laws of heaven here on earth. They are to throw themselves into the tasks of each hour with a disinterested love which is not one of the products of this time but a gift of the Eternal God.

From this three general conclusions may be drawn. First, the mission of the Church can never be founded on the works of social welfare which Christians perform. The publicity of missionary societies in past generations, which justified their work by their success in emancipating slaves, building hospitals and the like, placed the missionary motive in a false perspective. Our first responsibility is to proclaim the Gospel, to bring men to discipleship and witness. The social service of the Church must then grow out of this.

Second, on the other side, however, the Christian Gospel is in itself profoundly social. The attempt to bring an individual by his conversion out of the society of which he is a part is not only difficult, it is also not the way of evangelism which the New Testament shows. It is the task of the Christian evangelist to enter into the social structure which he seeks to bring to Christ, to penetrate the traditional customs (*adat*[1]) and transform them from within. It may be that the *adat* will continue to exist in a finer way because of this Christian penetration.

Third, against this background we must reconsider the old distinction between older and younger Churches. The implication of these words is that the older Church is strong, dominant and mature, whereas the younger Church is weak, childlike and not yet fully responsible. It may indeed be true that older Churches are strong and dominant, but this applies only to their historical and social position, not to their status as the Body of Christ. Their basic tasks and problems are not different from those of the so-called younger Churches. The concepts maturity and

[1] *Adat* means 'traditional customs'.

immaturity cannot be applied to portions of the Body of Christ. Thinking in terms of older and younger is essentially a product of the western mind. We are concerned today rather with the missionary responsibility of the whole Church toward the whole world. The national awakening of Asian countries requires that the connection between Church and mission be reconsidered in relation to new social structures, so that the Asian Churches acquire their own autonomy and responsibility. But the mission of the Church is a common mission. Christianity, which we formerly considered to be the religion of the people of the West, has now become a question and an invitation to everyman. Our experience with the Gospel in Asia reflects evangelistic problems in western countries too.

In the Asian situation, I would like to suggest that two problems for the Church are basic: (1) the establishment of an indigenous Church in the light of the real meaning of nationalism, and the proper regulation of missionary service from abroad in that Church; and (2) the deepening of unity between Churches of East and West in their common missionary task.

I. THE ESTABLISHMENT OF AN INDIGENOUS CHURCH

Our task here is beset by three dangers. The first is that the Churches of Asia may fail to communicate the Gospel to their own societies because they have learned the Gospel in borrowed words from the West. Borrowed words can be understood by minds intelligent enough to understand them, but they do not speak to the heart of a nation. They do not reflect its own spiritual struggles and therefore do not communicate the word of God.

Because missions cannot bear to lose their own background in the mission field it often happens that Churches springing from the respective missionary societies are more Methodist, more Anglican, more Reformed or more Lutheran than the mother Church itself. If there is a theological problem to be discussed, it is discussed from the denominational point of view and not from the point of view of Scripture. This has its roots in the old days, in Indonesia, when the Reformed Church was the only

Church allowed to disseminate Christianity. The Dutch East India Company was not only working for the Dutch government but also protected its Church and did not allow other Churches to be active. It was forbidden to pray for Christians in other areas. Everything to which the mother Churches were accustomed had to be planted in the daughter Churches. This era has now passed. The Churches of Asia carry their own responsibility for their message. Surely they should take steps to formulate their own confession of faith, liturgy, teaching and preaching, relevant to their own situation? Is it not the task of all Churches to be witnesses in their own environment and local traditions and release themselves from the traditions and background of the West?

The second danger is that we have been led to follow the clericalism of the Middle Ages and we are facing the possibility that the church may no longer be a 'spiritual home' but may be considered as a place to go for a service once a week. Because of this clericalism the people consider the church as the work and concern of the officers. This ruins our conception of the Church. In the younger Churches there must be no sharp divisions between preachers and laymen. In every church the laymen must feel free to express their minds, and it is for them to decide the means to show the pattern of their lives through their faith, so that the Gospel may be relevant to everyday life.

Thirdly, generally speaking the Churches have not yet realised their responsibility in the national awakening. Their time is more taken up with their own institutions than by the way of life of their own people. It is evident that if some members have turned their attention to politics they have rapidly lost contact with the Church. There are so many fields in which the Christian community can serve to help the victims of social and economic unrighteousness, to crusade against social disorder and to lead the way to the total change of society without violence in social and economic affairs. The sophisms of nationalism and Communism and the weak points of democracy must be illuminated, but negative criticism is not sufficient. We must not forget that the coming leaders of the East could be our own young generation. Their attitude toward nationalism, Communism and democracy depends on their own personal experience.

What action is needed to meet this new situation? Let me take an example from the experience of my own Church. At an early stage in its development it grew too quickly for the missionaries from abroad to be able to carry on all the evangelistic work themselves. This was especially true because the mission was also responsible for hospitals, schools and other forms of social service. The basic responsibility for the work of evangelism, teaching and baptizing was therefore given to the elders of the church who are ordained. They are now the kernel of each congregation. It is they who bring to fruition the plans of the church. Besides them there are school teachers and pastors, together shouldering a very big responsibility. Apart from the elders the heads of villages have also played an important role within the church activities: they have great authority but at the same time they also have great responsibility. People look upon them as holy men who make the sacrifices of the people and maintain the customs and laws of life. The group of elders meets regularly to discuss all the problems which are connected with spiritual life, pastoral care, education and church discipline. Nor do we apply western methods in seeking and training pastors. They are not appointed from among the young people but from the teacher-preachers who have had training and are eventually put into Pastor Training Schools. We select pastors from among the older teachers with good records and eight to ten years of practical work and give them a two-year theological course in both theory and practice. In addition to this training we try to communicate through special courses the meaning of their responsibility in the Church. But as new situations are coming up we are reverting to the western system, and we are now beginning to accept younger people for theological training. It is still a question whether this western system is better and more effective. It is giving us a group of leaders with a training similar to that of western missionaries, who can take over the administrative and teaching posts which missionaries formerly occupied. On the other hand, something is sacrificed of the pastoral wisdom which characterised the teacher-pastors chosen in the old way.

The question remains, what is the place of the foreign missionary in this structure of ministries in the missionary Church? It is our opinion that they should not become pastors in congregations. By so doing they hinder the development of the Church by their dominant influence. Nor should they be organised into a separate structure parallel to the Church and responsible to the missionary society in another country. Rather, they should come as brothers into the teaching and evangelistic work of the Church, and under its direction. Basically it is the Church which must carry on Christ's work. It is the Church which must involve itself with all its members in the affairs of the world, to manifest God's love toward the world. The foreign missionary is a symbol of the participation of the Church Universal in the work of the Church in one place.

Both clergy and laity have to learn their responsibility to witness in non-Christian movements. No Christian message can get deep roots in the East if the Christian way of life is not yet incarnated and a true Christian community set up. It is most important that the Church be aware of her own spiritual revival of missionary enterprise and that she teach a sense of eagerness for the inclusion of others in the Church. This eagerness should not only be limited to fellow Christians, it is for all who are in deep need without regard to group or class. We also have to take into account that western civilisation is misunderstood by eastern people because of Hollywood films, dancing, bars, and so on, and that the Christians do not have much time to look beneath the surface for the elements of Christian culture. In this tremendous task which confronts the Church today, good, theologically-trained ministers have a vital part to play in evangelism. Their approach to those areas still untouched by the Gospel should be more effective. The ministers have a vital part to play in evangelism. They have to be convinced that this evangelism is a tremendous task which is an integral part of the work of the Church. The world-wide preaching of the Gospel should be the responsibility of all members of the Church, the ministry playing a leading function in mobilising church activities. We want realism and statesmanship in leadership to enable the Church to confront all the challenges and obstacles. In the change of static feudalism into a dynamic democratic Asian world the Church must have corresponding leadership. The Church must live in and with the people imaginatively: it must seek to probe and understand the agonies, aspirations and longings for a better community life. The key factor in the twentieth-century situation is the rapid rise of the non-Christian and anti-Christian gospels. Our ministers have to be pushed into rural areas to work among primitive people, and into city areas to workers in the rapidly developing industrialised eastern nations. The increase of general education, the flood of modern technical and economic culture, the national awakening, the rapid change in social relations, secularism, nihilism, all have put us into a critical situation. It pushes us into more activities and it forces us to act with realism. If not, we shall miss the bus. Evangelism is not what man does in particular forms of activity, but what God does with anything we do.

2. THE DEEPENING OF UNITY BETWEEN CHURCHES OF EAST AND WEST

If we look carefully we can see that there is a unity between Asian and western Churches, and that is the *calling*. All Christians in a territory are called as one Church and by that calling they have responsibility, to answer to God for his calling to them. The western Church has been called to disseminate the Gospel and build up Christ's Church in an Asian place. Churches exist as the result of the Mission work. The Asian churches admit that the Mission called and supported them.

The Mission is like a pioneer and means for *oikumene*. As the Whitby Conference said, our Mission is an agent of the Church Universal, commissioned by one part of the Church for service in another part. The duty of the mission is to promote ecumenical understanding in the Church. As Hans Hoekendijk has said, the work of missions needs to be connected to a 'comprehensive approach,' including social and cultural activities. Mission work is a sacrifice offered by the Church, not of its own will and power, but under the will of him who owns the Church both young and old. In that case we see that it is the Church who calls the missionaries from abroad and it is within the right of the Church to decide or appoint who is to be called. We do not hinder those who want to come from abroad, but we must resist the pressure which still exists upon the missionaries in some areas from their home Churches to carry out the policies they desire and not what is best for the young Churches.

As new Churches, communities used to receiving help, we have to educate our people not to accept money simply because it is offered. We must teach that we have no right to accept money unless it is relevant at the point of our obedience. On the other hand, we must also teach the giving community that their giving cannot carry with it the right to control. While this is understood by mission boards and missionaries, it is doubtful whether it is realised by the members of the Churches who give. It is our task to educate these members not to give on the basis of pity or according to their own standards and values, but in obedience to God.

All Churches, new and old, must be one in him. Christ is not divided, and it is he who calls us all to obey and follow him. We are servants of the Lord. We have a Master. We receive our orders from him every day. We are here to bear responsibility to him, in one mission to the world throughout the world.

THE CHURCH IN THE WORLD:
THE UITLANDER IN NO MAN'S LAND

David M. Paton

'UITLANDER' was originally an Afrikaans term to describe those of non-Afrikaner origin, custom and language who had entered the Boer Republics of South Africa. It was suggested at Bossey by a Swiss missionary in South Africa that it succinctly indicated some at least of the dilemmas of the church worker (or the congregation) culturally and in other respects sharply distinct from the surrounding environment. 'No man's land' was originally used of the shell-pocked yards of land separating two hostile entrenched armies. It has been suggested by Bishop R. O. Hall in *The Art of a Missionary*[1] as a description of the peculiar realm, neither truly Chinese nor truly western, into which Chinese and missionary come to meet each other, and from which both retire (if they can) to their western or Chinese homes; and it can be used more generally.

'The uitlander in no man's land'—in a fundamental sense we Christians are all uitlanders, heirs of Abraham, children of the promise, seeking another country. Theologically considered, this world is a sort of no man's land, disputed as it is between God and his angels and the Devil and *his* angels; and, theologically considered, in so far as our true citizenship is in heaven, we must be uitlanders on the earth. This is the true strangeness, to which we are all called, individuals, congregations and churches alike; and we shall return to this calling before we finish.

In a second sense, also, there are those who are, as part of their Christian obedience, called to be uitlanders in the sense that God calls them to serve him in a country or a culture or a class not their own, and there to make the sort of home we mean

[1] SCM, 1942. This little classic, published in the USA as *The Missionary Artist Looks at his Job*, is, alas, out of print.

when we speak of the 'country of one's adoption'. At their best, such homes are places where two cultures can meet and enrich each other.

But there is also another, negative possibility. The burden of the critique alike of missions in Asia and Africa and of the bourgeois churches of the industrial post-Christian West is that they are uitlanders in no man's land in a further, disreputable sense, which conceals and may even destroy the reputable theological meaning. In brief, the Churches strike the Sheffield steel-worker or the African nationalist as 'foreign' not so much because they smell sweetly of heaven and in them resounds the music of Zion, nor yet because they have come from another culture with the mind in them that was in Christ Jesus to tabernacle among them, but because they stink of a class which he would condemn as bourgeois or of a nation which he would classify as imperialist, and seem largely undisturbed about it.

The unkind phrases are deliberate. There are indeed other and more favourable things to be said about the middle-class churches of the West and the mission churches of Asia and Africa; but they are perhaps too readily said by middle-class clergy and by missionaries. Should we perhaps not keep silent from self-praise, or even from self-defence, and allow God to be judge? Moreover, if we leap too suddenly to self-defence, we may miss important aspects of the truth.

These are matters that have been extensively discussed. Sardar K. M. Panikkar in *Asia and Western Dominance*[1] gives a very different—and much more 'Afro-Asian'—account of the relation of missions to imperialism than will be found in for example M. A. C. Warren's *Caesar the Beloved Enemy*;[2] E. R. Wickham's *Church and People in an Industrial City*[3] and R. H. T. Thompson's *The Church's Understanding of Itself*[4] dissect the religious life of Sheffield and Birmingham in a way which calls in question the usual assumptions of conventional parish strategy.

In this essay one cannot hope to do more than to open up one

---

[1] Allen and Unwin, 1953.   [2] SCM, 1955.
[3] Lutterworth, 1957.   [4] SCM, 1957.

or two of the more personal aspects of the situation of the church worker and the congregation and the Church as it is found today in both East and West. We shall consider first 'foreign-ness' in the East, and then one of the reactions to it, the 'Christian Movement'; secondly, we shall ask whether tendencies of the same sort cannot be detected in the West; this will lead us to some reflections on the delicate problems that arise between leaders and led; and this will lead us finally to a consideration of the perils of 'objectivity'. So far as I know there is no considerable body of published material on these themes which will allow of objective scientific general statements; and the method must perforce be at times autobiographical. In my own case it happened that my missionary apprenticeship for the most part was at the hands of Chinese rather than missionaries; and that I embarked upon the charge of a working-class English parish without either previous English parish experience or any formal theological training. In so far as this experience is a-typical, it has probably had the usual results: that one sees some things with extra clarity and misses some things altogether. But of that others are the best judges.

THE UITLANDER IN NO MAN'S LAND: IN THE EAST

What in the first place is the purpose of one's work? To preach the Gospel and to establish or build up the Church, as God gives us to do these things? But unless we happen to be among the minority who are genuinely pioneers, and this minority is today a shrinking one, we find ourselves in confused situations where the ultimate aim easily becomes remote. Missionaries may remember uneasily Henry Venn's phrase about the object of the mission being the euthanasia of the mission; and this or some similar formulation is now widely accepted: but do our activities really suggest it? In the years immediately after the war money was poured into the work in China, and little more result was achieved than a partially successful attempt to restore the *status quo ante bellum*. In the hindsight of the years after 1949—and the revolution in the affairs of the Chinese Church is far from over—

it must be judged that this money was largely wasted—worse, it may even have made things in the long run more difficult.

The central problem here of course is that we had lost the sense of a coherent decisive purpose in the light of which priorities might be not only determined in council but kept to in action: we were, in effect, reduced to keeping things going. We must return to this point, but it is worth pausing to draw attention to the fact that the things, often good in themselves, that we create acquire in the course of time a momentum of their own. The school is there and must be kept going, even if, in circumstances which have become quite different from those of its founding, it has but the most tenuous link with the life of the Church. The money has been given, and we feel we must spend it, even if the purpose for which it has been given is one that we should not budget for if we were budgeting for our needs with a clear head and a free hand.

Institutions, and the money with which we sustain them, are potentially instruments of our central purpose; but they can too easily escape and set up as it were on their own, much in the way that in parts of Christendom the sacraments of the Gospel seem to have escaped from the Gospel and become almost self-sufficient and almost magical. There can come a point when the sacraments cease to express and represent the Gospel and become a substitute for it. There can come a point when the physical apparatus of the mission has taken over, and concealed or even destroyed the central purpose of the mission.

This is later reflection. At the time, we sought to keep things going; our attitude to the continuing monuments of past glory, our use of present money, was symbolic, it now seems, of an attitude in which a coherent discrimination of priorities had been lost. The ultimate aim had become remote.

Wherever this happens, there is evidence of a theological and religious failure—a failure to see clearly and to act whole-heartedly. But this was not the only source of confusion, of that atmosphere in which almost everything becomes a 'problem'—and a 'problem' is, by unstated definition, a matter to worry about without expectation of conclusion. The other source is our ambiguous relation to, our fuzzy understanding of, the environment in which we are set. We have called this 'no man's land'. We do not, most of us, get very close to grips with the substance of the land of our adoption; and the more successful the mission has been, the wider and deeper the penumbra it creates round it of a culture that is neither the one thing nor the other: neither a genuine outpost (futile as that would usually be) of western Christian culture, nor truly indigenous.

The root of our difficulty here is not the fact that we are not trained sociologists or anthropologists or what not, but that it just does not seem terribly important to take our environment seriously. It was my privilege during some of the war years to serve as the foreign member of a team of student secretaries in National Central University in its makeshift war-time campus outside Chungking. All who did work of this kind were amazed that it should be possible for there to be official, open Christian work actually centred inside the campuses of the great Government universities; but I doubt if we missionaries took this Chinese university world anywhere nearly as seriously as did our Chinese colleagues. We tended to think them a bit faint-hearted in their evangelistic attitude; was it rather that they had a more sensitive respect for this part of God's world, even if it did not yet know him?

Churches which were dominated by missionaries, Churches which felt western rather than Chinese, Churches which failed to communicate the words of Jesus in accents recognisably his, Churches which were aloof from national shame and national aspiration—we need not stay to argue how far these impressions were true in China or are true anywhere else. This, is, crudely put, the sort of impression that 'the Churches' make on many people all over the world, and it is not surprising that there is a reaction.

A REACTION: THE 'CHRISTIAN MOVEMENT'

F. B. Welbourn in a penetrating essay on 'The Missionary Culture'[1] suggests that the 'separatist' Churches of Africa are one

[1] In *Essays in Anglican Self-Criticism*, ed. David M. Paton (SCM, 1958).

of the African responses to the confused contact of the culture of the 'Christian-scientific-industrial West' with the local African culture. Another consequence which seems to demand far more discriminating and sympathetic attention than it has so far received, is what in China used to be called 'the Christian Movement'. My own first, decisive, experience in China was in the YMCA and therefore within the centre of 'the Christian Movement'; but it is only as time has passed, and I have been able to reflect upon the experience of fifteen years ago in the light of much more recent conversations with Chinese, and with people from other countries, that the deep significance of 'the Christian Movement' in relation to the Churches has become clearer to me.

It was the phrase used by a good many educated Christians in the circle of the YMCA and YWCA and the universities to describe what they belonged to; and its significance seemed to be mainly negative—in a rejection of the Church as foreign, and of its orthodox faith as incredible and, because apparently indifferent to the tragic frustrations of China, reactionary. Those who sought a positive point of view found it in the 'Social Gospel', which facilitated a combination of religious concern for politics and society with detachment from the institutional Churches and from, in particular, orthodox Christology. The men and women of the Christian Movement were passionately concerned with national affairs and national politics, especially as these were focused in successive student movements, and were on the whole politically very Left-wing. It is surely of great importance that the 'existential' choice for many sensitive young Chinese within and without the borders of the Christian Churches has for some decades been between Christianity and Communism, and that a creative minority has for decades accepted the Marxist analysis of the contemporary world even if they have become in the end members of the Church (and indeed clergy) rather than officials of the Party; and surely the inability of so many of us western Christians even to be able to understand how people can ever be *tempted* to become Marxists, or even thorough-going nationalists, is one of our severest handicaps in understanding the rising educated

48

minorities of Asia and Africa? We are like moral welfare workers who cannot understand 'how girls go wrong', frustrated before we start.

If the Christian Movement was preoccupied with politics, it was bored with theology. 'Theology' was simply a lot of irrelevant abstractions. In so far as theology came into the picture, it was not orthodox but heretical; so far as words went, this judgment was correct. A further differentia of the Christian Movement from the Churches was that missionaries were on the whole peripheral: the Y's and the Christian universities were led largely by Chinese and sensitive to China; many people in them owed no decisive experience of Christ to the ambassadorship of a missionary.

But as the war years passed, there came a change. In wartime West China, we began to talk theology. In this context to believe theology to be important, but to have had no formal theological training, was a positive advantage; it meant that what theology once had had been acquired because it was needed and not because its study had been necessary for a degree; if one was carrying lumber about at least it was one's own fault. This interest in theological issues did not, I think, grow out of war-weariness and the depression that characterised those years. Is it not more likely that our Chinese friends had already begun to perceive that in the civil war which from 1940 onwards became increasingly the real war, the Communists were likely to win, and that as a consequence the missionary-Christian world would be largely swept away (as it has been), and therefore that the Chinese Church would be itself responsible to God both for the purity of the Church's faith and for the intelligibility with which it presented the faith to the Chinese people? Theology then would no longer be something peripheral, but something central; no longer a matter that could be left to missionaries, but a matter for the most earnest Chinese attention.

At all events the situation now appears to be that it is precisely where Christians are most preoccupied with the role of the Church in the service of the Chinese people that they are most concerned with theology; and the schism, if that is the right word, between Christian Church and Christian Movement is on the way to being healed.[1]

This particular experience may perhaps be tentatively, generalised in the following form. The 'Christian Movement' is the correlative of the 'uitlander' in 'no man's land'; a 'foreign' church makes for 'unchurched' Christians. But is the phenomenon solely Chinese? Is the 'No Church' movement in Japan[2] a similar kind of phenomenon? Is the falling-away from the Churches on the part of educated West Africans, for example, due to straightforward worldliness (as in part it doubtless is—anywhere)? Or is it a more important, ambivalent, phenomenon than that—a rejection of irrelevance in the name of a deeper religious commitment, even if this last has not yet become explicit?[3]

THE UITLANDER IN NO MAN'S LAND: IN THE WEST

Cannot these things be seen in the West too—indeed is their presence in the East not in part due to export from the West? Are we clear about our purposes, our priorities, in the West? Does the average Christian congregation—or for that matter the outstandingly successful one—generally suggest to the outside observer the priorities of the Gospel? If he studies its activities, and the importance actually attached to them, does he feel that he is inspecting a colony of heaven, a limb of the body of Christ, entrusted with his mission to the world? It is unfair to ask whether the congregation is 'aflame with zeal for souls' because it is unfair to suggest that *any* congregation of sinful men, even if they be believers, will be corporately aflame about anything for very long at a time; the drag of the world, the flesh and the devil is strong

[1] As also perhaps the tension between 'liberal' and 'fundamentalist'.

[2] See 'Non-Church Christianity in Japan' by W. H. H. Norman, *International Review of Missions*, October 1957.

[3] It is only too likely that this summary and selective account of the Christian Movement will be held to be inaccurate and misleading alike by Chinese and by missionaries; candour should prompt the admission that it is different from the assessment that appears in my *Christian Missions and the Judgment of God*. But I do not think it is wrong to urge that we seek for the positive significance of movements of this kind; or to believe that if we do this, we shall learn a great deal about ourselves that will remain hidden as long as we are content to classify them as Christian deviations; or to feel that the process may take some time.

on all of us, even the saints. Corinthians, Galatians, Thessalonians and the rest knew all about them, and were far from model: who are we to expect to be different? But are not our noticeboards revealing? Superficially, they suggest[1] that we are almost entirely concerned with money and with ways of raising it. This surely is a libel: the average congregation is *not* primarily concerned with money, though its church council may sometimes be. The noticeboards reveal not so much apostasy as confusion—confusion about priorities, about the order of importance of various matters in the Christian scheme of things.

Nor can one be sure that in the West the Churches are truly related to the people among whom they are called. In Britain—or at least in the Church of England—one of the great questions for clergy is the real nature of the people of England who refuse either to 'come to church' or to be excluded from 'the Church'. From this point of view the perennial discussion about whether or not we should be 'rigorist' about the baptism of the children of people who are not apparent believers or the marriage of divorced persons with partners still living is a debate between opposing understandings of the religious state of the English people, and if the debate is inconclusive or at least not yet concluded, this is not only because we have not yet agreed about the theology of the questions, but also because we have not yet set ourselves to patient understanding of our *milieu* in a spirit of loving detachment—the spirit in which one is loved by, and tries to love, parent or brother or spouse. Such love sees far more, not less, than is revealed without love; and it is not blind.[2]

---

[1] At all events, in Britain.

[2] It is a significant illustration of our theme of the unity-in-mission of East and West that more than one English reviewer of *Essays in Anglican Self-Criticism* picked out J. V. Taylor's essay on 'The Principle of the Conditional Administration of the Sacraments' which is based on the experience of the Church in Uganda as being of the first importance for the 'baptismal rigorism' discussion in Britain. By the same token, his full-length study, *The Growth of the Church in Buganda* (SCM, 1958), the first of the International Missionary Council's Studies in Younger Churches, is both an admirable example of the candid and loving study of a Church and its environment, and also full of suggestiveness for those who work not in 'the mission field' but 'at home'.

And so it is not surprising that here too we have our analogue of the 'Christian Movement'. For how else are we to regard such a one as the late John Middleton Murry, that deeply sensitive intellectual, loving Christ and (whatever one's reservations about some of the theology of his *Life of Jesus*) meeting him with a more radical honesty than most of us orthodox professional Christians contrive? Unable to escape from Christ, or to be happy in his Church as he found it, at one time near to Anglican ordination, and then deciding that the most relevant response to the distresses of our time was to be found in the development of a Christian community on the land, and yet at the end of his life an elected member of the church council of the village church, Murry is surely representative (not of course in detail but in Christian substance) of very many people in our time.[1]

A few paragraphs back, we mentioned the Corinthian Christians to whom St Paul addressed those long letters, apparently intending them to be read to the church assembled for worship and fellowship. One could ask the most searching question of all in the form: could our congregations have fundamental doctrinal and ethical points put to them as a body in the expectation that they would respond? It was not only that he put fundamental things to them; but also that he expected of them responsible decision. It may be doubted whether in East or West we shall get much straighter about these things—about the purpose of the Church and the purpose of the professional within that purpose—until we ask far more searching questions, ask them, as it were, from within the Bible, and ask them together. I suppose most people who are likely to read this book also read the Bible and read it regularly, but is it not astonishing, when one thinks about it, how little our corporate Christian life, as congregation, as mission, has in the assumptions of its policies been brought under the discipline of Holy Scripture? This was Roland Allen's cry, contrasting the missionary methods of St Paul with our own: I hardly think we

---

[1] See *Not as the Scribes*, 'lay sermons' by Middleton Murry, edited by Alec R. Vidler (SCM, 1959).

have yet accepted it where it hurts most and is most difficult—in our committee discussion and decision.

Let us say then that we have to worry away, like a dog with a bone too large for its teeth but nonetheless determined to get at the marrow, at the question what it means, in this *milieu* where I and mine now are, to receive from God and develop for ourselves and others the *ecclesia* of God, the fellowship which he creates and in which we are together in Christ.

LEADERS AND LED

This leads us naturally to our third subject: how do we think of 'our people'—those firmly within our fold? In particular, are they objects of our pastoral or evangelistic activity, or subjects in their own right? Missionaries in a foreign land, clergy of an alien class, inescapably we professionals have some sort of leadership and responsibility thrust upon us, however much we seek identification, trying not to be as painfully noticeable as a sore thumb but to take our places as part of the landscape. However far the recovery of the doctrine of the laity goes, pastors and masters, ministers of Word and Sacrament remain. (Indeed, in the troubled parts of the 'Deep South' of the USA, the ministers are by and large far ahead of the laity in understanding what most of the rest of the Christian world understands to be the plain implications of the Christian faith for race relations; and this is evidence that the Church positively *needs* some leaders who by the very fact that they *are* professional clergy are to some considerable extent shielded from the pressures that may tyrannise over the laity, to match the evidence of the damage that is done to the Church when its leadership is almost entirely professional.)

Missionaries are peculiarly aware of the embarrassments of talking about their work. It is not only that it is felt, perhaps wrongly, that the people 'at home' to whom we speak cannot stand overmuch of the truth, and want above all to hear of the miseries of the pagan world and of the triumphs of the Gospel; or that if they avoid these excesses, on the whole and perhaps not unnaturally they want to hear about 'our missionary', and one is forced therefore subtly or far from subtly to distort any situation but that of a pioneer mission in its very early stages. Is it not also that so often one would not wish what one says to be overheard by or get back to the fellow-Christians about whom we are speaking? And am I wrong to believe that a good many Asians and Africans are uneasy if not positively resentful about a good deal of our deputation work, and that their feelings are not without reason?

How is one to think of one's flock? Sentimentally?—'they are wonderful people'. 'Realistically'?—'they are hopeless!' (One of the most lifelike touches, as it seemed to one spectator, in the film of Alan Paton's *Cry the Beloved Country* was that at some point or other all the 'do-gooders', clerical and lay, black and white, lost heart and cried 'These people are hopeless'.)

Perhaps it is an error, or a source of error, to suppose that one has to come to any *conclusion* at all. Is it our duty to try to present our people 'objectively'; may we not perhaps be called to try to say what we can of what we think they would say if they were to be their own representatives to another part of the Church instead of acting through us as their proxies? In my own case, I left China in 1950, convinced that it was my calling to try to say the kind of things my bishop and his colleagues would want their western friends to hear, to explain what it felt like to be them—rather as one who, seeing one member of a far-flung family after a visit to another, passes on the family news. At times, there was no news, and one steered by dead reckoning (there are times when one has not the foggiest idea what is going on in the mind of brother or sister—and times when they seem to be drawing away from one). But then one would hear again. I know that I have never ceased to belong in some way to the Chinese Church, have never been able to speak or write in complete unawareness of what they might have to say about it if they heard me, have tried to think more in terms of 'us' and less in terms of 'them'; and have all the time been also aware that I might be doing the job so badly that the day might come when the Chinese Church would disown me, if in fact it has not already done so.

THE PERIL OF 'OBJECTIVITY'

There are occasions, however, for thinking that this sort of approach has a more general validity. History does not suggest that men immersed in tense situations make the best objective reporters. One does not go to Laud for an objective appraisal of the Puritans, to Luther for an unbiassed account of late medieval Roman Catholicism, to Peter Canisius for a detached scholarly account of Protestantism. Moreover, the rewriting on the western side of the history of the Great Schism between East and West (for example, in Steven Runciman's *The Eastern Schism*)[1] now makes it clear that the difference of political system was an overwhelmingly important 'non-theological factor'; that much trouble was caused by the habit on both sides of treating partial information as if it were complete, and putting upon it the most unfavourable interpretation; and that the West on the whole was more guilty of this than the East—a Russian friend is charitable enough to ascribe this difference to the fact that the Byzantines had a better civil service. So far as China is concerned, are we not falling into the same errors, with the danger of the same sort of schism in the future? At all events, one person at least came to believe that his own calling was to do what he could to present matters as the Chinese see them, eschewing the task which belongs finally to God, and mediately perhaps to the anthropologist, the sociologist, and the historian, of offering an objective account of what is happening in China and of the relations of Chinese and western Churches.

But more generally, is our enthusiasm for 'objectivity' in this context justified? Is it not significant that it is only in these years, immediately before the tercentenary in 1962 of the Act of Uniformity, 1662, establishing the Church of England and prescribing the Book of Common Prayer 'and none other' for public worship, that Anglican and Free Church scholars can together in co-operation set about the task of composing an authoritative history of the religious struggles of seventeenth-century England?

[1] Oxford, 1955.

At this lapse of time, that task should be possible. But if it has taken 300 years to reach objectivity about the seventeenth century, can we who are in the midst of things expect to be objective about the twentieth?

In any case, are we not all subjects, whether we be 'uitlanders' in some more or less alien environment, or genuinely natives in a culture to which we belong? Is there not an important Christian truth about us here? And, as a matter of fact, is not the best 'missionary writing'[1] that which contrives to present with some success the flavour and atmosphere of some other part of the Church than that to which we belong? Are we not in fact at our best when we are being, with the utmost truth and love, fully 'subjective'? And does not this apply equally to the kind of writing which seeks to describe and communicate some fresh initiative in worship or evangelism in a European or American church?[2]

'Here', says the Scripture, 'we have no continuing city'—and who in this age of sputniks should feel this more acutely than the minister and the missionary whose work takes him from one culture into another so that he belongs to neither fully? If one was brought up on the humanities, one is tempted to foreboding where men of science and technology see shining vistas of opportunity. If one comes from the West, one wonders in our late-imperialist age what place there will be for the 'white' man in two or three generations—or earlier—but it is idle to expect Asians and Africans to share our fears. If one contemplates the disintegration of the old geographical certainties—Latin America is Roman Catholic, Sweden is Lutheran, Burma is Buddhist, Egypt is Moslem—one wonders what will happen when Rome really gets to work in Scandinavia, or Buddhism in Britain, or Protestantism in Latin America—and trembles perhaps overmuch for one's private Ark of the Lord. The new patterns that are beginning to emerge may have little or less or quite different room for

[1] As notably J. E. L. Newbigin, *A South India Diary* (SCM, 1951).
[2] For example, Tom Allan, *The Face of My Parish* (SCM, 1954); E. W. Southcott, *The Parish Comes Alive* (Mowbray, 1956).

the missionary and the professional minister as we have known them.

We find ourselves recalled to Abraham. One hears surprisingly little about Abraham in the pulpit, considering how his name crops up again and again at critical moments in the Gospels and the Epistles. But is he not the 'paradigmatic man' for us? When he was called, he went out (as we must) into a country he did not know; and there he was to receive (as we shall) an inheritance. And perhaps if our faith is as Abraham's, and we become more detached from bondage to our history (as he had to be from the culture of Mesopotamia), we shall find that our problems yield and our divisions are healed.

THE RESPONSE OF ISLAM TO THE IMPACT OF THE WEST

Arend Th. van Leeuwen

'In religion, in morals and in politics it is now the fashion to believe one thing and to profess another. It is reckoned a virtue or wisdom to suppress the truth, if not to profess what you hold to be a false opinion. I have the privilege of knowing a gentleman, a Mohammedan by profession, who owes his success in life to his faith. Though, outwardly, he conforms to all the precepts of Islam and occasionally stands up in public as the champion and spokesman of his co-religionists; yet, to my utter horror, I found that he held opinions about his religion and its founder which even Voltaire would have rejected with indignation, and Gibbon with commiserating contempt. But it is not he alone who thus wears the cowl of sanctity. There are hundreds besides who count hypocrisy as a venial sin and falsehood a pardonable weakness.'

Mr S. Khuda Bukhsh, of India, who wrote down this indignant exclamation in his *Essays Indian and Islamic* before the first world war, expressed one aspect, and certainly not the most manifest and dominating one, of the response of the Moslem world to the western impact. At that time European interest in Islam focused mainly on the question whether Islam would be able to adapt itself to western civilisation. The French rationalist, Renan, in a well-known study, *L'Islamisme et la Science* (1883), bluntly denied the capacity of Islam to reproduce the spirit of modern science, and Lord Cromer, the brilliant administrator of Egypt in the first decades of British interference, tersely summarised his judgment in the statement: 'Islam cannot be reformed; that is to say, reformed Islam is Islam no longer; it is something else' (*Modern Egypt*, 1908). But the first world war, with its uprooting consequences in eastern countries, opened the eyes of many western critics to the remarkable political vitality of Moslem populations. Since then we have grown accustomed to thinking of Islam in terms of 'revival' and 'renaissance'. The rising tide of eastern nationalism, the birth of independent Moslem countries after the second world war, and the way the Moslem peoples are realising their possibilities and power today, are rapidly changing the face of the Moslem world.

It is, however, easier to describe the face value of this revitalisation process than to gauge what is really happening beneath the surface. Terms like 'revival', 'renaissance', 'reformation', 'renewal', on the one hand, and 'crisis', on the other, are too cheap, and run the danger of becoming nearly meaningless, if we do not penetrate into the actual—partly paradoxical—content of this terminology. There are three factors which may be too easily overlooked. First, there is more continuity with the past in the renewal of the Moslem world of today than we are apt to assume. This remark does not refer to the evident tenacity of age-old conservatism, but it draws our attention to the everlasting problems these attempts at renewal have to face—everlasting because they are inherent in the religious system of Islam. Second, the 'reformation' of Islam at the present time is for the most part a reaction to the western impact, and only in a very secondary sense does it receive its inspiration from original sources. And third, what we are facing today is only the beginning of the encounter between Islam and western civilisation. It is an open question whether a real encounter has already occurred, and in any case the time has not yet come, and may never come, to talk about a 'crisis of Islam'.

Within the limits of this chapter we can only focus our attention on three aspects of this encounter: *secularisation*; *Christianisation*; and *modernisation*. The first two derive their meaning especially from the western factor in the encounter, while the third aspect outlines the Moslem reaction. But this is only a question of emphasis, because what we have to describe is an interchange of action and reaction, not isolated structures.

I. ISLAM AND SECULARISATION

'Islam cannot be secularised,' answered a professor at the Al Azhar University when I had a talk with him in Cairo about the dangers which are menacing the position of any religion in the modern world. To a certain extent he was perfectly right. It is perhaps the deepest enigma of Islam that it is so unconscious of its own original and essential secularism, which has in fact immunised it against the glaring effects of secularisation which have undermined the religious foundations of western culture. It is this secular spirit which blinds the eyes of pious Moslems to the real and fatal threat of secularisation. The central problem of Islam is its capacity for being at once deeply religious and thoroughly secular, while remaining completely heedless of the contradiction in this condition. Yet, instead of acknowledging its dilemma, it is proud of what it considers to be a comprehensive virtue of combining heaven and earth, the divine and the human, in one religious system.

The gentleman whose free-thinking ideas so repelled Mr Khuda Bukhsh conformed *outwardly* nevertheless to *all* the precepts of Islam. The crux of this statement lies not so much in the evident hypocrisy of this Moslem as in the words 'outwardly' and 'all'. 'All the precepts of Islam' is the same as: *the Canonical Law of Islam*, the *Shari‘a*; that is, the total content of its theocratic system, 'the rights and duties', in the words of a famous Moslem definition, 'whereby man is enabled to observe right conduct in this life, and to prepare himself for the world to come.' This legal system is not 'law' in the modern sense. Its basis is (1) the revelation in the Koran, supplemented by (2) the authoritative traditions of the Prophet, and further supplemented and cemented by (3) the infallible consensus of the community. It is God's Law, which cannot be rationally analysed or understood, for it is *ta‘abuddi*: it has to be accepted by man as God's *‘abd* (servant), irrespective of its seeming contradictions and incomprehensible precepts. As God's Law, it exerts, by its very nature, a comprehensive rule over all aspects of life: religious, political, social, domestic, individual. The second part of its precepts, which deals with the juridical and political domain, is completely equivalent to the first part which refers to the ritual-religious duties, and the same applies to a host of exact precepts concerning social and cultural manners and customs. For the fundamental purpose of the Shari'a is in the first instance the theocratic domination of all life, and only in a secondary sense the determination of juridical relations.

Evidently, this totalitarian religious system could not help meeting with strong opposition. The first resistance pertains to the *outward* character of the Shari'a; and two other points of opposition are concerned with its *all*-inclusiveness. The enormous influence of mysticism in the Moslem world is partly understandable as a necessary reaction against the exclusively external character of the Shari'a, which leaves the personal relationship with God in the religious conscience to every individual, to determine of his own accord. Mysticism intruded, to satisfy the deeper religious need of the human soul, and in the course of the centuries the Sufi brotherhoods spread ever more widely and drove their roots ever more deeply into the soil of Moslem life. Even in its orthodox form this meant a serious encroachment upon the absolute character of the Shari'a, for this mystical religiosity is actually an escape from the strict interpretation of the Law, because it considers the outward precepts as only the first step on the path of the mystic, which finally guides the religious seeker into the lonely heights of mystic communion with God. This does not necessarily mean hypocrisy, but it has accustomed the average Moslem to a problemless acceptance of the habit of mental reservation. Moreover, this mysticism has in practice been strongly mingled with all degrees of popular magical beliefs.

The second opposition originated at a very early date and has deeply affected the history of development of the Shari'a. It was an unavoidable reaction against its totalitarian pretensions. The revelations of the Koran did not include a legal system, but resolved a series of questions which occurred incidentally during Mohammed's life. Mohammed's successors in Medina, the first four Caliphs, could not continue the prophethood, but they combined a living knowledge of the Koranic precepts with a real political and juridical power. The situation changed after this initial period when, under the Umayyad Caliphate, the centre of government moved to Damascus. The jurists lost their influence on the actual life of the political community and began to build up a legal system on the basis of the Koran and the Tradition, which was hardly in touch with the real situation of Islam. The distance between the ideal Shari'a which was built up by the jurists into an ever more detailed casuistry, on the one hand, and the real development of political life, on the other, became unbridgeable. The impracticality of this ideal legal system was acknowledged by the jurists themselves in their pessimistic statement that the Shari'a could only be realised in the golden period of the first four Caliphs and in the eschatological period of the coming Mahdi. Theoretical observance was, however, the duty of every Moslem. The political government would readily pay this tribute of theoretical acknowledgement, but in practice it put its own ordinances through and maintained its civil courts alongside of the Shari'a courts, whose jurisdiction was finally limited to the sphere of ritual-religious obligations (including marriage, personal and family relations, inheritance, endowments), which was closely connected with the popular religious conscience. The political and administrative institutions, a large part of penal jurisdiction, and most large-scale commerce lay under the authority of the secular government. With regard to constitutional law, international law, and the law of war, the Shari'a has never been in force. This glaring contradiction between religious theory and secular practice is especially reflected in the history of the Caliphate, which according to the regulations of the theologians should succeed the Prophet in government, conduct of the holy war, and jurisdiction, but in reality, after a rapid secularisation, gradually lost its power, became a puppet in the hands of rival governments, and, after the end of the fourteenth century, chanced to be usurped by the Turkish Sultanate, whereby even the strictly Arab prerogatives of the Caliphate were violated.

Beside the political power there is another element in the situation which resists the comprehensive authority of the Shari'a, viz. the customary law (*'adat; 'urf*). Although this has never been accepted in legal theory as one of the foundations of the Shari'a, it is a fact of enormous importance, and throughout the Moslem world the actual observance of those legal ordinances which have practical meaning (ritual duties and personal relations) is to a great extent dependent upon its conformity with the traditional customary law.

In this undeniable contradiction between the ideal pretensions of the Shari'a and its very limited real position, there has remained, however, in the course of the history of Islam, one fact of overwhelming importance: the *theory* has never been affected. It is at this point that the impact of western civilisation has introduced a new element which has confronted Islam with an unprecedented situation. Our Indian Moslem, who only outwardly followed the Shari'a, was not at all an unfamiliar phenomenon in Islam and certainly no cause for alarm. That he conformed to all the precepts of Islam was an overstatement which no Moslem could interpret otherwise than as his theoretical acknowledgement of the totalitarian rights of the Shari'a. What caused the indignation of Mr Khuda Bukhsh was, therefore, not the hypocrisy of his co-religionist, but the fact that this gentleman fostered ultra-Voltairian ideas about his religion and its founder, which could not help, in the long run, undermining and destroying the ideal foundation of Islam upon its divine Shari'a.

It is not accidental that the extreme consequences of this unavoidable effect of the western impact have been drawn in Turkey. The French Revolution began to exert its influence in this country even before the beginning of the nineteenth century, through the legal and social reforms of the Sultan, which were continued by several of his successors in the course of the nineteenth century. A new middle class arose, consisting especially of army officers who had received French training, and government officials. A new literature, imbued with the French spirit, spread ideals of *Watan* (fatherland), *hurriyet* (liberty), *Khalkdjilik* (democracy), *meshrutuyet* (constitutionalism). The rapid spread of education under the influence of French missions and stimulated by the founding of government schools resulted in the proclamation of the first constitution in 1876, an abortive attempt at liberalisation which was annihilated by the reactionary tyranny of Sultan Abdul Hamid II. The growing opposition of the new bourgeoisie burst out in the Young Turk Revolution of 1908. The Ottoman Empire remained, however, a Moslem state. The Young Turks attempted the impossible, in striving after three mutually contradictory ends: Nationalist Turkism, maintenance of the decaying Empire under the banner of Islam, and parliamentary constitutionalism. Turkey's defeat in the first world war spelt the death of this unrealisable attempt.

The dilemma in which Islam found itself between the ideals of nationalism and liberalism, imported from the west, is manifest in the teachings of one of the most interesting intellectuals of that period, a forerunner of Kemal Atatürk: Ziya Gökalp, whose daring plan of reform was based on his interpretation of Islam as a purely ethical religion. The Islamic customary law, which has never been accepted by the Moslem jurists as the fifth basic principle of the Shari'a, was proclaimed by Gökalp as a 'divine revelation'. On this basis he advocated far-reaching religious reforms: first, to separate religion and state, in order to put an end to the domination of Islam over the political and social life of the Turkish nation; and second, to separate religion and oriental civilisation, and thus to make possible the maintenance of the fundamental values of Islam side by side with European civilisation and Turkish national culture. This programme, which has in many respects influenced the formation of the new Turkey, he summarised in the threefold ideal: 'Türkleshmek, Islâmlashmak, Muasirlashmak' (Turkification, Islamisation, Modernisation).

In the utter emergency of the catastrophe of the Ottoman Empire at the end of the first world war, the Turkish nation could not, however, be saved by theories, but only by the political genius of Kemal Atatürk. This man was a convinced atheist and completely unromantic. From the very outset he had the clear insight that it was impossible to separate Islam from the ruined empire. Not the Ottoman Empire, but only the Turkish domain could be saved; and therefore Islam was bound to fall, together with the Ottoman myth. In his nationalism he was radically matter of fact. The romantic dreams of the unification of all peoples of 'Turkish race' he rejected as sheer folly; under the pressure of hard political facts there was only Turkish Anatolia which could exist as an independent nation. Thus from the threefold programme of Gökalp and of the Young Turks there remained only the ideal of modernisation (westernisation), and the point of Turkification was limited within the boundaries of a politically possible national existence. 'Our religion is extremely rational and natural. A natural religion has to conform to the laws of reason, science and logic.' Thus declared Atatürk in 1923, a year before he decided to abolish the Caliphate.

The radical secularisation of the new Turkish state was an affair of Turkey alone, although other Moslem countries had their comments on this experiment, which they observed with mixed feelings of surprise, aversion and admiration. The abolition of the Caliphate, however, was more far-reaching in its consequences and provoked reactions throughout the Moslem world. At this point one effect of the western impact became manifest: that it disturbed the veil of the sacral *theory* and confronted Islam with hard facts. What no Moslem had had the courage to say was revealed by the simple decision of an atheist Turkish president: that the Caliphate had long since degenerated into a mere fiction. Ziya Gökalp had dreamt of saving this sacred institution: 'In order to create a really effective political unity of Islam, all Moslem countries must first become independent: and then in their totality they should range themselves under one Caliph. Is such a thing possible at the present moment? If not today, one must wait. In the meantime the Caliph must reduce his own house to order and lay the foundations of a workable modern state.' But the Caliph was unable and unwilling to reduce his house to order; he took refuge with Turkey's enemies and tried to ruin the initial modern state. And Turkey, now independent, was bound to decide that it could not afford to bear the burden of an institution which it considered as the enemy of its progress for the sake of a fictitious theological doctrine only. Ziya Göpalk had suggested leaving the Caliph in a position of spiritual leadership, similar to that of the Pope in the western world. But this comparison was utterly false, and contrary to the essence of the Moslem Shari'a, which does not acknowledge a separation between religion and state.

Thus the abolition of the Caliphate was the source of great confusion. Its basis was in the third source of the Shari'a, the infallible consensus of the Moslem community. A congress was convened in Mecca, only to reveal that a consensus of the community was at this point non-existent, let alone infallible. Was it not wiser, then, to acknowledge the impossibility of the restoration of the Caliphate and to adapt theory to the logic of hard facts?

This was what was actually done by the great Moslem poet and philosopher, Sir Mohammad Iqbal. He recognised that the Caliphate had long since lost its real power. Far from serving any useful purpose it really stood in the way of a reunion of independent Moslem states. His conclusion is that 'for the present every Moslem nation must sink into her own deeper self, temporarily focus her vision on herself alone, until all are strong and powerful to form a living family of republics'. What is, however, this 'deeper self'? Iqbal expresses his great admiration for modern Turkey, who 'alone has shaken off her dogmatic slumber and attained to self-consciousness. She alone has claimed her right for intellectual freedom; she alone has passed from the ideal to the real.' But this intellectual freedom resulted not only in the abolition of the Caliphate, which Iqbal placidly accepts, but in the initial separation of religion and state, which he rejects, because, as he rightly declares, it contains a dualism which does not exist in Islam. His ideas are confused at this point of first importance. We should not forget that Mohammad Iqbal has become the spiritual father and national hero of the largest Moslem state of today, Pakistan, which maintains Islam as the state religion.

The question which Iqbal could frankly discuss in Moslem

India, where the intellectual middle class enjoyed a rather independent and free position in relation to the religious authorities, aroused vehement repercussions in Egypt, which centred around Shaikh 'Ali 'Abd Al Râziq. Born in 1888, he was one of the first to enjoy a secular western education at the new Egyptian University at Cairo, and later studied economics and political science at Oxford. After his return he was appointed a judge in the Shari'a courts. In 1925, a year after Turkey's abolition of the Caliphate, he published in Arabic his book *Islam and the Fundamentals of Authority*. He argued that the Moslem world has no need for the Caliphate. Mohammed did not attempt to found a state. His authority was merely spiritual and not political. The Shari'a, which he brought, was only concerned with religious affairs and did not have in view the regulation of civil affairs.

The book was bitterly assailed by the religious leaders. The Azhar Court passed sentence on the author and dismissed him from the body of the *'ulama* (religious leaders). It was all too evident that the thesis of this book—the separation of religion and state and the abandonment of the Shari'a as a civil code—was in flagrant contradiction with orthodox Moslem theory. This book reveals the tragedy of a displaced intellectual, who is neither at home in his own religion nor in the west. For all his eventual sympathy with this courageous Shaikh, no western Islamist could possibly support his views on the history of Islam, nor accept the arbitrary scientific method by which he reaches his conclusions.

It is easier, however, to dismiss a heretic Shaikh than to quell the issue which he has raised. The Azhar-shaikhs have never been able to offer any acceptable solution to the riddle of the Caliphate, the abolition of which they rightly reject as incompatible with orthodox theology. But what is more serious is that in defending the theory they completely neglect the contradictory position of Islam in their own country. For the Constitution which Egypt was able to proclaim in 1922, in its new independent status, confessed Islam as the religion of the state, but was for the rest one convincing proof of the impracticality of the Shari'a in a modern state: canon law was largely ignored by the Constitution.

Not every Moslem, however, is able to shut his eyes to the manifest contradiction between the sacred theory and the plain facts of civil life. The rebellious movement of the *Ikhwân-al-Muslimîn*, the Moslem Brotherhood, is one of the most startling evidences of the enormous bewilderment which results from the penetration of western civilisation. The movement owes its widespread following throughout the Near East partly to the general social, cultural, economic and political malaise, which is particularly felt by the urban intellectual and semi-intellectual classes. That may explain its extremist ideology, which turns it into an enemy of the government, and its vehement xenophobia. But there is another side of the medal too: its downright orthodoxy. The movement is an ardent protest against the incompatibility of a modern constitution with the totalitarian claims of Moslem canon law. It accuses its government of consisting of hypocrites who behave as good Moslems and pretend to govern their country as a Moslem state, and at the same time display in their measures and ordinances a frightening contempt for the most fundamental claims of the Shari'a; and it aims at replacing the present heretical regimes by a really and truly orthodox constitution, which acknowledges the Shari'a as the total foundation of civil affairs. This nostalgic ideal of restoration of the golden period of the Prophet is not, however, felt by the *Ikhwân* as reactionary. On the contrary, Mohammed's regime was for them the unsurpassable model of real progress, in comparison with which all achievements of western civilisation are but pitiful imitations. Return to the original Moslem theocracy will therefore automatically bring back the splendid period of political power, and liberate Islam from its abject serfdom to western imperialism. The Moslem Brotherhood is, in its theocratic extremism, a necessary outlet for the mental pressure experienced by those orthodox Moslems who feel that they have fallen victim to a foreign penetration whose spirit and aims arouse their deepest aversion, because they cannot help admiring its power.

Is there a way out of this dilemma? There is one Moslem country, which has recently won its independence, Indonesia, where the experiment of a kind of middle course has been adopted. The Indonesian Republic is neither a secular nor a Moslem state. The ideological basis of its draft constitution is the fivefold principle of the *Pantjasila* (an old Javanese, Sanskrit term, which means: five principles), which only remotely resembles the 'Six arrows' of Kemalist Turkey (republican, nationalist, populist, statist, secular, revolutionary), the secular principle of which it emphatically rejects. The five principles of the *Pantjasila* are as follows: 1. *Ketuhanan Jang Maha Esa*; 2. Respect for human values; 3. Democracy; 4. Social justice; 5. Nationalism. The second to fifth principles inclusive are quite 'normal' foundations for a modern state. The crux is the first principle. *Ketuhanan Jang Maha Esa* means: Almighty and One Godhead. This rather vague term (*ketuhanan* is a neuter, derived from *Tuhan*—God) was purposely chosen so that the connection between state and religion might be maintained without proclaiming an Islamic State. In the Draft Constitution this principle is closely linked with religious liberty, and President Sukarno has officially interpreted it as 'tolerance'. The average Moslem, however, tends to explain religious liberty as a corollary of the political freedom Indonesia has acquired: Indonesia's religion—i.e. Islam itself—also requires freedom. Moslem apologists consider Islam as the guarantee of true religious liberty, and therefore the more orthodox among them tend to explain this first principle as a plain confession of Islam as the state religion. This arouses serious suspicion in some secular quarters and among Protestant Christians.

The hybrid character of this vague religious foundation becomes evident at the very point where it has to be put into practice. The Republic of Indonesia possesses a Ministry of Religious Affairs, a compromise between the theory of complete separation of religion and state and the theory of unity of religion and state. In reality, however, the Ministry has gradually grown into the instrument whereby Islam is more and more woven into the general pattern of state organisation. It has *in nuce* the structure of an Islamic State. Indonesia's promising attempt to steer a middle course is not, in fact, a solution to the dilemma, but a typical expression of an age-old Indonesian concept of society. This is also transparent in the fact that only in this country the *adat* (customary law) has been accepted by the jurists as a more or less official foundation of the Shari'a.

Several Indonesian Moslem authors have tried to give a theoretical basis to this middle course policy in describing Islam as an 'ideology'. One of the outstanding Moslem leaders, Mr Muhammad Natsir, former Prime Minister and chairman of the big Moslem political party, Masjumi, argues in his writings that no state whatever can be built up without an ideological basis. In western countries the basis of the state, often made explicit in the Constitution, is the Christian religion. He maintains that Islam, although it rejects a separation of religion and state, has never known a theocratic system in another connotation than that state and government are recognised as part of the divine world order. This means 'that religion must live in every individual follower of the faith and therefore pervade the life of the community and find expression in statehood, government, and legislation, never, however, losing sight of the fact that there are worldly concerns, on which the people decide for themselves.'

Evidently this evasive formulation can mean all or nothing. We meet the same ambiguous trend of thinking in a stricter philosophical presentation, in the lectures of Muhammad Iqbal, already mentioned above: 'The state, according to Islam, is only an effort to realise the spiritual in a human organisation. But in this sense any state not based on mere domination, and aiming at the realisation of ideal principles, is theocratic.' Indeed, Orthodox Moslem leaders in Indonesia openly declare that the vague religious basis of the Indonesian Republic is not essentially at variance with the foundation of Pakistan as an Islamic state. Vis-à-vis western criticism and under the influence of western political philosophy, a process of spiritualisation of theocratic theory is taking place in various parts of the Moslem world, which enables Moslem leaders to evade painful questions with regard to the real position of the Shari'a, while enforcing the all-pervasive influence of Islam over all spheres of life.

2. ISLAM AND CHRISTIANISATION

Islam has, from its very outset, been a rival to and an enemy of Christianity. As a consequence there developed a vast and elaborate apologetic and polemic literature, which launched its ingenious attacks on Christian theology, especially on Christology and on the authority of the Bible. The Christian Churches answered these attacks in the same controversial style.

This sort of apologetic has not disappeared. But in general it has retired to a background position and has made room for a different mode of combat, the weapons of which have been determined by the western rival in the arena. We should never forget that the penetration of western civilisation into the Moslem world was extremely painful to the Moslem consciousness, because it included the unprecedented and impossible superiority of Christianity. The glory of Islam and the seal on the truth of its revelation has always been its initial defeat of vast areas of the Byzantine Empire, its Christian adversary. In the Middle Ages Islam was again able to withstand the series of attacks of the Crusades. This equilibrium has been disturbed by the expansion of modern western imperialism. The Moslem mind, which essentially thinks of religion in political terms, could not but experience this penetration as a scornful defeat by its Christian arch-enemy. The western impact therefore was bound to result in a change of attitude on the part of Islam, so that the counter-attack which had formerly focused on Christian theology was now to be directed against western Christian civilisation. This reaction was to a great extent also due to the attitude of Christian missions, which were unwittingly exerting a far more extensive influence as a vanguard of modern cultural ideals than in their right presentation of Christian doctrine. Evangelisation, both in word and in deed, was a permanent criticism of the miserable decay and the backwardness of Moslem civilisation as such, rather than on account of its falsity. The absolute norm of revelation was gradually replaced by the standard of humanitarian idealism.

The reaction could not fail to come. The rising new middle

class in India was the first in the Moslem world to reach the intellectual level needed to supply the right counter-plea. In 1891 Amîr 'Alî published his *The Spirit of Islam*, which has become an almost classical model of counter-attack against the unbearable pressure of the pretensions of modern Christianity. The book extols Islam for its spirit of tolerance, its concern for social justice and its promotion of enlightened scholarship, cleverly using nine-teenth-century historical-critical analysis of the origins and history of Christianity to illustrate its utter failure in all these spheres. Amîr 'Alî not only defended Islam and restored its severely shocked self-respect, but he was able to present a brilliant and impressive picture of its superiority to Christianity in all aspects of modern civilisation.

This circumstantial apologetic work of a learned, modern-educated Indian Moslem, although it was primarily intended for his own countrymen, had to some extent also a western audience in view. In the Moslem world its influence has not been rivalled, to the present day, by any other apologetic study. Ten years later, in 1901, the leading Egyptian modernist, Muhammad Abduh, published a study in Arabic, comparing the two rival religions: *Islam and Christianity in their attitudes to learning and civilisation.* The foundations of Christianity are described in seven points: 1. It believes in miracles; 2. It has no freedom for investigation, for belief is fixed by the power of the Church; 3. It is a monastic religion; 4. It encourages belief in the unintelligible, in defiance of the law of reason; 5. The Bible is believed to contain all that men need for living, so that from the very beginning the Church has been opposed to learning; 6. Following Jesus, who taught the hatred of one's own parents, wife and children, Christianity is aggressive towards non-Christians; 7. It separates the Church from state, culture and society, which are left to their old pagan spirit.

How different is the picture of Islam. This religion, on the contrary, 1. Is based on rational thought; 2. Affirms the priority of reason over traditional teaching; 3. Is slow to accuse of un-belief; 4. Demands belief in God's universal laws of nature and has led to all kinds of scientific investigations; 5. Rejects priestly, dictatorial authority; 6. Uses force only in case of self-defence; 7. Encourages respect for other religions; 8. Does not separate religion and world, but comprehends harmoniously this world and the hereafter. Here again, the religion of Islam is pictured as the champion of all that a modern Moslem values and admires in modern culture and society, while Christianity, in glaring contrast with its wholly unwarranted pretensions, is the enemy of progress and science.

One more example of this present-day reply to Christianity: a pamphlet by an Indonesian writer. A leading Indonesian politician and economist, Mr Sjafruddin Prawiranegara, wrote some years ago during the revolutionary struggle for independence a small but interesting study, entitled *Islam amid the tribulations of the World* (*Islam dalam pergolakan dunia*), which presents Islam as the 'third power' between Communism and Capitalism. He analyses the development of Capitalism as an unavoidable result of Jesus' teaching of complete self-denial, which in practice gave tyrants and exploiters a free hand to oppress their fellowmen. Marxism has been a necessary reaction and protest against this exploitation of the masses. But in contrast to Christianity, the religion of excessive love, it fell into the other extreme and became the message of eternal hatred. Between these two opposites, Islam is the golden middle course, teaching neither impractical love nor devastating hatred, but realising the combination of respect for one's neighbour with a manly defence of one's rightful interests. Thus Islam asserts in modern times its original proclamation of being the final and ultimate religion for the whole of mankind, as the successor of Judaism and Christianity. While Christianity has resulted in the system of Capitalism, the opposite extreme of Communism is the product of Judaism, for Karl Marx was a Jew, whose teaching is the echo of old Jewish ideals. Thus history is repeated, and once again Islam will save this world, torn asunder by the evil results of the two rival religions, and will proclaim world peace in mediating between the two extremes of its predecessors, Judaism (now Communism) and Christianity (now Capitalism).

This socio-religious philosophy of history is a remarkable

attempt of an Indonesian Moslem intellectual of today to conceive Islam as the ultimate religion in God's design for mankind, the only hope for a bewildered century. Against this eternal background the Indonesian struggle for independence and its policy of neutrality between the big powers attains the final significance of a saving message for the whole world. The new trend in apologetics, which judges Christianity not according to its theology but according to its pretensions to be the foundation of western culture, confronts us here in a conspicuous form.

3. ISLAM AND MODERNISATION

Modern Islam is in the first instance a phenomenon of reaction to the intrusion of western civilisation. The term 'Moslem modernism' is an invention of western observers and more a sign of embarassment than an adequate definition. In so far as the term might suggest the existence of a clearly definable political or social movement, or a philosophic trend, which has rallied round the banner of a unifying ideology, it is a misleading description of what is really going on. Moreover, in some of its prominent representatives this modernism is not 'modernist' at all, either by European, or certainly by Moslem standards. We cannot, however, dispense with this terminology, for it is the inescapable indication of a gradual change in the spiritual climate of living, thinking, feeling, acting and reacting in those circles and centres of the Moslem world which have made contact with the West and have more or less undergone its influence. Uncohesive, ambiguous, full of inner tensions and contradictions, their mentality feels more at home in the emotional sphere and resists rational self-clarification. If it reaches the level of formulated self-expression at all, it is generally accessible in hundreds of pamphlets and small booklets, and even in more voluminous works it seldom puts on airs of systematic and fundamental thinking.

There are two countries in which Moslem modernism first centred, to spread later throughout the Moslem world. In each of these countries, India and Egypt, it originated in rather different circumstances and has assumed a rather different form.

India was the first country, mainly owing to the British policy of extensive western education, where clear attempts were undertaken to reshape Islam in a new fashion, and these initiatives have gone further than anything in Egypt and the Near East. Although at first it was the Hindus who for the most part profited from these new opportunities, there gradually grew up in the second part of the nineteenth century a new Moslem middle class, which was dependent on the British Government and began to model itself on western patterns of life and thinking. This new class of Moslems was dependent on British capitalist imperialism for its function, and was itself without religious forms and ideologies suited to its changed way of life. The first major development in Moslem modernism, therefore, was the working out of a liberal Islam, compatible with the nineteenth-century West, similar to it in general outlook and, especially, in harmony with its science, its business method, and its humanitarianism. This was done by extracting principles from the body of the law and concentrating on them exclusively, purging the religion of feudal manifestations, and discarding as later accretions or misinterpretations all that hindered or ran counter to western bourgeois principles. The outstanding figure in connection with this phase is Sir Sayyid Ahmad Khân (1817-98), founder of the Anglo-Oriental College in Aligarh (1875), whose aim was to combine religious education and the best Moslem cultural traditions with modern scientific studies. The College, which was supported both by the Moslem bourgeoisie and by the British Government, became the centre of dissemination of modern ideals and has exerted a great influence. The following year Ahmad Khân began an Urdû commentary on the Koran: a radically new interpretation of Islam and its Scriptures in the light of nineteenth-century rationalism. An Urdû journal, modelled on British examples, was founded by him as an organ of humanitarian reforms among his co-religionists. At the same time he devoted his attention to the need for apologetics, for which purpose he wrote in English his *Essays on the Life of Mohammed*, an attempt to prove that Islam is a respectable religion, judged by modern western standards.

At the end of the last century Moslem modernism was gradually entering a new phase, of which Amîr 'Alî is the main representative. As the Moslem middle class became less dependent and more a rival to the British bourgeoisie, its self-reliance with regard to its own religion became more aggressive. Modern science and civilisation were now said to be derived from the glorious Moslem culture of the past. Intense interest was devoted to the image of Mohammed as the supreme character of all history, the model of all virtues a modern man can think of.

But when Amîr 'Alî died, in 1928, the Moslem bourgeoisie had already begun to fall a victim to a growing frustration. Many educated men had discovered that the present condition of society did not offer them the opportunities they had reckoned with. There arose an increasing tendency to repudiate not only the West, but also Westernism itself, and to supersede liberalism by a new creative vision for the future. This phase ended, during the last decade before the second world war, in the frightened reaction of communal fanaticism of which the birth of Pakistan has been the final result. The hero of this recent phase is Muhammad Iqbal (1878-1938), mentioned above. His education in England and Germany led him to admire greatly the immense vitality of European life and to see its tremendous possibilities. But for all its values, Europe could not be to him a model of perfection. Especially its capitalism he considered as the main cause of its materialism and irreligious character. He returned to India with a new and vibrant message, which centred round a revolutionised Islam, in opposition to the attitudes of eastern resignation and passivity. Influenced by Nietzsche and Bergson, he gave expression to a radically new interpretation of the Koran, which in reality turned Islam into a specimen of irrational, mystic humanism. That the emphasis here was really on the salvation rather than the revolutionising of Islam is borne out by Iqbal's deep-rooted conservatism with regard to practical reforms, and his championship of the self-defence of a political collectivism which resulted in the making of Pakistan.

A remarkable characteristic of this more advanced Indian

modernism is the fact that it is led by laymen: chiefly officials, lawyers, propertied men and university teachers. Here we find the reason for its free and often daring trend of thinking. Evidently, these intellectuals need not look cautiously backward to the impelling censorship of the conservative theologians. They master the English language and feel at home in western literature. The independent educational centre at Aligarh has given a powerful organisational support to the movement. But there is also a weakness here. Professor Gibb, in his enlightening and critical analysis, *Modern Trends in Islam* (Chicago, 1947), has pointed to a striking difference between the Christian West and the Islamic world. Whereas, in the West, it is very largely the theologians themselves who are reshaping religious thinking in terms of the prevailing philosophical and historical ideas, the vast majority of orthodox *'ulama* (theologians) in the Moslem world cling to un-bending conservatism. They defend Islam without knowing the modern world which they are defending it against. On the other hand, the average middle-class apologist does not really know the Islam which he claims to be defending, and he defends instead an imaginative reconstruction on liberal lines which he passion-ately believes to be the genuine teaching of the Prophet Moham-med. This modernism may be attractive, encouraging, sometimes brilliant, but it is without real authority and foundation in the orthodox structure of Islam. This explains why the aversion of orthodox conservatism towards these modernising speculations is so deep-rooted and, from the Moslem theological point of view, so justified. But it is an overstatement when Professor Gibb concludes that Moslem modernism is 'primarily a function of western liberalism'. The tragedy is that it is neither orthodox nor liberal. It is a repercussion of the intrusion of a set of fragments of modern western civilisation. Whereas western liberalism is a certain phase in the development of a whole culture, this Moslem modernism is uprooted, without real spiritual background. In contrast with nineteenth-century liberalism, with its increasing historical-critical sense and its unsparing attack on the foundation of Christian doctrine in the authority of the Bible and the revelation in Christ, Moslem modernism lacks any really scientific basis in its apology for Moslem history, and, for all its criticism of the authority of Tradition, it deals with the divine character of the Koran and with the person of Mohammed as though it had never heard of even the possibility of religious and intellectual doubt. There are only very few signs of slight awakening in this direction.

In Egypt there has developed a type of modernism which is rather different from the advanced modernism in India. A fact of first importance is that here the initiative was born within the circles of the orthodox theologians themselves, centred in the ancient Azhar University at Cairo. These men had little or no knowledge of modern languages, and their understanding of western civilisation was very superficial. Their mental climate was the traditional Moslem culture and theology. That had its great advantages. These men really knew the religious system which they were eager to dress in modern fashion. They were actually not 'modernists', but they called their movement *Salafiyyah* because they wanted to restore the original Islam of the *Salaf*, the first generation. In this ambition they would only continue the puritanical reform movements of former centuries, which also had launched their attacks on all sorts of heretical innovations and had called the Moslem community back to the simplicity of the original revelation. Back to the Koran! Muhammad Abduh and his pupil published a voluminous Koran commentary, in which they tried to re-interpret the holy book in the light of modern thought. Muhammad Abduh undertook courageous attempts to reform the educational system of the Azhar University, but even his moderate proposals met with the tenacious resistance of orthodox conservatism. In the course of time, however, this modernism has gradually pervaded the orthodox atmosphere. It owes this relative success to the fact that it was itself a branch of the orthodox tree. As compared with the advanced trends of Indian modernism this Egyptian movement was very conservative. It rejected with indignation all attempts at re-interpretation of Koran and Tradition which went further than its own concepts, like the work of Shaikh 'Ali

'Abd ar-Râziq, mentioned above. With regard to the question of the status of women in Islam, for instance, it tried with great caution to interpret the Koran in favour of monogamy, without denying the lawfulness of polygamy. The suggestion of the Indian modernist, Amîr 'Alî, that 'before long a general synod of Moslem doctors will authoritatively declare that polygamy, like slavery, is abhorrent to the laws of Islam', could only be rejected by these Egyptian theological 'modernists' as wholly unwarranted and fantastic. On the contrary, Rashîd Ridâ has written an ample apology for the institution of polygamy against western criticism; and he has advocated the restoration of the Caliphate.

This Egyptian modernism has a vast influence throughout the world of Islam, from North Africa to Indonesia. On the whole it has become a paramount instrument to maintain the traditional structure in a seemingly up-to-date fashion against all secular criticism. Pretending to build a bridge between Islam and the modern world, it is in reality a symptom of the rift between the two. Mohammed rejected Christianity. In the following centuries Islam had to face the encounter with autonomous Greek thinking, and orthodox theology succeeded in defending its position. In the challenge of modern western civilisation the two devils return in a monstrous alliance, and with immeasurably refined technique they have begun their attacks on all fronts. 'Moslem modernism', properly speaking, is a collective noun for a variety of trends of thought among all those Moslems who have begun to realise that the traditional defence against Christianity and against Greek thinking does not meet the needs of the present time and who therefore look for new and safer positions. It is also the diagnostic term for the insoluble dilemma of a culture and society involved in an ever-increasing conflict between deep-rooted orthodox tradition and turbulently uprooting secularism. Western Christians may have their thoughts about this phenomenon, but they are certainly not in a position to evade the hard fact of their fundamental solidarity with their fellow-men in the Moslem world, now passing through a revolutionary age.

BIBLIOGRAPHY

Of the vast quantity of literature on modern Islam only a very limited selection in the English language can be mentioned.

Kenneth Cragg, *The call of the minaret* (Oxford, 1956).

Kenneth Cragg, *Sandals at the mosque: the Christian presence in Islam* (London, 1959).

H. E. Allen, *The Turkish transformation: A study in social and religious development* (Chicago and Cambridge, 1935).

Uriel Heyd, *Foundation of Turkish nationalism: The life and teaching of Ziya Gökalp* (London, 1950).

S. Khuda Bukhsh, *Essays Indian and Islamic* (London, 1912).

J. M. S. Baljon, *The reforms and religious ideas of Sir Sayyid Ahmad Khân* (Leiden, 1949).

Sayyid Amîr 'Alî, *The spirit of Islam* (4th ed., London, 1956).

Mohammad Iqbal, *The reconstruction of religious thought in Islam* (London, 1934).

Wilfred Cantwell Smith, *Modern Islam in India* (London, 1946).

C. C. Adams, *Islam and modernism in Egypt* (London, 1933).

H. A. R. Gibb, *Modern trends in Islam* (Chicago and Cambridge, 1947).

Harry Gaylord Dorman, *Toward understanding Islam: Contemporary apologetic of Islam and missionary policy* (New York, 1948).

W. F. Wertheim, *Indonesian society in transition* (The Hague, 1956).

THE GATHERING UP OF HISTORY INTO CHRIST

J. E. Lesslie Newbigin

In Europe, in the United States, in Africa, in the Islamic world and in India we are meeting situations which are extraordinarily different one from the other, and we must be careful to avoid the temptation to try and bring them all under one heading and indulge in premature simplifications. Because I am living and working in India, it is inevitable that my approach should be shaped by the situation as it is in India. And there, it seems to me, in contrast with much of what seems to be happening in other parts of the world, we have a situation which is primarily characterised by a kind of serene confidence, a conviction that the future belongs to us. Certainly we can say that it is characteristic of the Indian situation at present that immense new forces have been released and are being exercised. It is a very moving thing to see village people turn out to build their own roads, schools, wells, instead of sitting back and asking the government to do it. That is something new, and a symptom of the release of new forces which is taking place in India today. But at the same time we are not having in India the disintegration of social life or of thinking which is taking place in some other parts of the world. That is partly because of the extreme toughness of the Indian caste system which has retained its essential strength and thereby preserved the individual from atomization. And on the other hand it is due to the extraordinary toughness and comprehensiveness of Hindu thinking, especially the fundamental pantheistic theology of the Vedanta. Hindu pantheism seems to be able to absorb modern science and technology without even suffering from mild indigestion. 120 years ago, when there was a great debate in India between orientalists and occidentalists, i.e. between those who advocated Sanskrit as the language of education and those who advocated

English, the latter were quite convinced that the use of English would mean a total revolution in Indian life and thought. When Duff started what is now the Scottish Church College in Calcutta teaching little boys English literature, language and philosophy he was asked what he was doing spending his time in these things instead of preaching the Gospel. He said, 'I am laying a mine which, when it explodes, will blow up Hinduism'. The mine has exploded, but Hinduism is still there; for Hinduism is not a granite block, but a sandbank.

And yet at the same time, underneath the surface, there is no doubt that there are changes taking place which will eventually have profound effects. It seems to me that what is happening is an irreversible change in human thinking which is being brought about and which is causing men to make demands of life which they have never made before—such demands as the demand for certain fundamental human rights and the demand and the expectation that this world shall be made a place more secure and more comfortable than it has been for our ancestors. These demands are being made as a matter of course, and this leads on to the complex political and social changes which lead in the direction of the welfare state, the socialist democratic state, which India is building today. That is the sort of background out of which I am speaking and which must necessarily affect the way I look at the whole problem.

Now I ask how we are to understand this whole immense variety of changes which we see as we look at the modern world in East and West, in the old Christendom and in the areas outside that old Christendom. I don't think that merely by observing the multiplicity of phenomena we are going to find a pattern in them. Our task today is to take the biblical understanding of the world, and see how far it gives coherence to the multitude of different impressions we have as we look at this variety and changing scene. The thesis that I want to argue is this: that what we are witnessing is the process by which more and more of the human race is being gathered up into that history whose centre is the Cross and whose end is the final judgment and mercy of God.

A very long time ago, before I was a Christian, I read Myers' *The Dawn of History*. The first chapter of that book is called 'The people who have no history', and it was a reminder of the fact that vast periods and areas of human life have no history. Although human beings have lived and died and probably fought wars and done all the things that human beings do do, nevertheless they have no history. Nothing was felt to be happening significantly and therefore nothing has remained which we can call history. But it seems that what is happening now (I am not an historian, much less a philosopher of history) is that the peoples who have no history are being drawn into the history of which the centre is Jesus Christ; and that is the only history. In other words, that which has been static, or at least cyclical, in which the only movement was round and round, life and death, rise and fall—that is being drawn into a movement which is linear and dynamic, which is moving irreversibly and can never be back where it was before. The ferment of change which arises from the impact upon the ancient cultures of the Gospel, or at least of that kind of life which has its origin within Christendom, is the force which is giving an irreversible direction to that which was static or merely cyclical. When I say the impact of the Gospel or of that kind of life which has its origin in Christendom, I include technology, western political ideas, Communism—all those things which have come into the eastern world from the West and have their roots in the Christian tradition.

I want to suggest that we must interpret this drawing together of all peoples into an irreversible movement in terms of the apocalyptic teaching of the New Testament, in terms of the fact that world history is in the grip of Christ, is being propelled by him towards its ultimate issues, propelled through tribulation and conflict to a final consummation in which the judgment and the mercy of God which are set forth in the Cross are finally and conclusively worked out. We will not arrive at any such pattern by simply looking at the facts. We can only proceed by going to the New Testament and asking there what the pattern is, and then by taking it to the facts and asking how far it interprets them. I simply want to share with you some of the perhaps obvious things which stand out in my mind after reading the New Testament to see what it says about the world and the nations, with this particular issue in mind.

Fundamentally the New Testament gives us all the time a profoundly paradoxical interpretation of the world. We can try to express that in six different ways, all of which bear upon the same paradox:

1. The world belongs to Christ and yet it is in the power of the devil. The wise men from the East bring their offerings, acknowledge as it were on behalf of the world the kingship of Christ, but it is the devil who offers Christ the kingship of the world and says that it is in his power to offer it. Or as the same thing is expressed in John: the world was made by him but the world knew him not. The world is his but the whole world lieth in the evil one.

2. He has come to save the world. God was in Christ reconciling the world to himself. He is the Saviour of the world. He has come not to judge the world but that the world through him should be saved. And yet on the other hand his coming is the judgment of this world. His flesh is bread for the life of the world and yet that very offer of his flesh as bread for the life of the world brings judgment. It is at the point where that offer is made that many disciples go back and walk no more with him and one is identified as a devil (John 6.60-71).

3. He came to gather all into one. 'I, if I be lifted up from the earth, will draw all men to myself.' The Good Shepherd gathers all the sheep into one flock. And yet his coming provokes the hatred of the world which hates him and his disciples. Over against the Christ there emerges the figure of the Antichrist, the false counterfeit of power and grace and wisdom, gathering multitudes, deceiving even the elect. The story of the things to come is the story of an increasingly fierce struggle between Christ and Antichrist, culminating in the final struggle and victory. The figure of Antichrist does not, I think, play a very large part in modern Christian writing—at least in English; but that figure

emerges in an odd way, in unexpected places. In Orwell's *1984* Big Brother is Antichrist, the one who offers salvation to the world and whose offer is accepted by the vast multitude, and that reminds one of the unforgettable fragment of Soloviev: 'A Vision of Antichrist'. And that again reminds us of the book of Revelation and its interpretation of the Roman Empire with its offer of *salus* for the whole world, of peace and security of the whole world, as the Antichrist. And the relevance of that to our own day and to the ambiguities of the welfare state is very clear. In every case the point is that the essence of the Antichrist is that he looks like Christ, so much so that even the elect are deceived. He looks like the answer to every human need, looks like the universal saviour. According to the New Testament, world history has to be understood as an increasingly acute conflict between Christ and Antichrist.

4. Christ calls all people out of the world, but he sends people into the world. There is an absolute separation between Christ's people and the world. 'They are not of the world even as I am not of the world.' But at the same time there is an absolute identification. They are being sent into the world. They are in the world. They are the salt of the earth. In the same way there is an *ecclesia*, a body called out of the world to be the bearers of God's purpose in the world, but the end is not a Church but a city, and a city in which there is no temple. The end is not a restored Church but a new heaven and a new earth, a restored world.

5. This people which is chosen out of the world by God is at the same time judged by the world for its apostasy. You will recognise that as a constantly recurring theme in the Bible. The world which knows not God knows God better than the Church which knows God. 'I have not found such faith, no, not in Israel. But many shall come from the East and the West. The men of Nineveh will rise up at the judgment with this generation and condemn it. The Queen of the South shall rise up at the judgment with this generation and condemn it.' And listen to this from Paul, quoting Isaiah: "I have been found by those who did not seek me; I have shown myself to those who did not ask for me." But of

Israel he says: "All day long I have held out my hands to a disobedient and contrary people" (Rom. 10.20-1). And moreover, according to Paul, God uses the obedience of the heathen to provoke to jealousy his own disobedient people. 'I will make you jealous of those who are not a nation, and with a foolish nation will I make you angry' (Rom. 10.19). Surely that has relevance for the world today: God uses the obedience of the heathen to provoke his own disobedient people.

6. Christ is the final judgment of the world; all men and all nations are ultimately judged by their relationship to him. And yet Christ is hidden in the world, hidden so that even his own people do not recognise him. 'When saw we thee hungry . . . ?' Christ is hidden in the world, Christ is the judge of the world. To meet Christ we have to go into the place where apparently he is not, i.e. into the world which lies in the hands of the evil one.

I have done no more than to give an untidy summary of the things that struck me as I read the New Testament with these issues in mind and asked the question, what is the world, what are the nations ? Let me not attempt to sum it up. I have no tidy conclusions to offer, but offer these four thoughts:

1. The world is in Christ's hands and it is his purpose to bring the world to the final issue of mercy and judgment. As we see in the Gospel story our Lord bringing his disciples gently, patiently but inexorably to the point where they have to face the final issue of faith or unbelief in him, so we see him leading the nations of the world. We see nations being drawn out of isolation and stagnation, into one unitary historical process of which the central issues are being determined by the whole complex of ideas which derive ultimately from the revelation in Christ. They may derive at many removes, but the point is that we are now witnessing the reality of world-history, of a unitary history. And that means that the question of the relation of every man to Christ is becoming more and more inescapable, more and more inevitable, more and more central. One could illustrate that interestingly from India. In the midst of what I described at the beginning, i.e. the fact that Hinduism appears to be able to digest the whole of western

technology, science and religion without indigestion, we come across this document, the Niyogi report produced by Madhya Pradesh. It is now evident that the beginnings of indigestion are to be observed. Some intelligent people are beginning to realise with a shock of horror that Christ presents them with an absolute decision. Over and over again the report prints in horrified italics the statement that Christ is seated at the right hand of God. These are distinct signs of indigestion. The terrible fact is beginning to be clear that in Christ you are presented with a claim to absolute kingship. This report is one of the most encouraging things that has taken place in India for a long time from the missionary point of view. It shows that the real claim of Christ is beginning to be heard. There is a beginning of a meeting between the Gospel and the Hindu mind. One could look at the leaders of the Gandhian movement in India and one finds in them men very, very near to Christ and very, very far away at the same time, men who are profoundly attracted and fascinated by the New Testament, who read it and re-read it, and who are trying with an obedience far greater than that of the vast majority of Christians to follow Christ and yet rejecting the claim that Christ himself makes. Here again is God using the obedience of the non-Christian to provoke the Christians. Such men are trying to follow Christ with devotion and self-sacrifice, and yet rejecting the claim of Christ to exclusive Lordship. In some of the most sensitive spirits in India today, men who are playing a crucial part in the development of the nation, you have this evidence of our Lord leading people right to the ultimate issue of absolute surrender or final rejection. They are far away from the cyclical, self-contained life of that which is not yet history; they are caught up in an irreversible movement. What you see in these men is a sign of what is really happening to the world; that what we are witnessing is the process by which more and more of the human race is being gathered up into that history whose centre is the Cross.

2. We have to be awake to what the New Testament says about the Antichrist. That which looks most like the offer of salvation may

in fact be the farthest away from it. Again I think of the issues being raised for India by the development of a socialist democratic republic essentially along the lines of a welfare state. The demand for such a kind of state arises ultimately from Christian sources, from that valuation of the human being which the Gospel has introduced into the world as distinct from the conception of the human being of pre-Christian Hinduism. But it makes demands that ultimately only the Gospel can meet and it therefore seems to me that it leads us closer to the issues of Christ and Antichrist. Every time there is a step in the direction of totalitarianism, there is the fundamental question of the value of the human being as such. The issue Christ-or-Antichrist is going to be pressed harder and harder upon the conscience of every man.

3. We need to be aware of that paradox which I tried to express by saying that Christ is hidden in the world, the world which lieth in the hands of the evil one. We shall not meet with Christ except by going right into the world, into the very situations where it appears that Christ is being denied. I have in mind again such issues as we are facing in India in the sphere of education. A very great effort is being made to convert the whole elementary educational apparatus of India into that form of basic education worked out by Gandhiji. That involves many of the insights of the Gospel with regard to the education of the human being. But it is also intimately tied up with the Hindu conception of religion which ultimately excludes the possibility of Christianity. The most honest of the leaders of Indian education will confess that their ultimate object is a society in which a religious minority is unthinkable. To that end the basic education schools make it a fundamental part of their programme that there should be common worship in which the resources of all religions are pooled and students are trained so that they cannot make an exclusive claim for any one religion. The Church is faced with the alternative of staying out of that situation because of the fear of compromise, and thereby losing any opportunity to make a concrete witness not only in the training school of today but in the India of tomorrow and thereby becoming irrelevant to the national life;

or on the other hand of trusting in the power of the Holy Spirit to guide one and going into that situation at the risk of making grave mistakes in order to be sure that we are there to bear our witness where men and women actually are. We have to take seriously the fact that we meet Christ in the world, even hidden in the world, at the point where his own people do not recognise him.

4. In the first Epistle of John where these themes of the world and of Antichrist are most explicitly dealt with he comes down very heavily on this emphasis: 'Jesus Christ come in the flesh', the concrete humanity of Jesus. This emphasis is absolutely crucial for our obedience in the world if my understanding of what is happening is at all true. 'Jesus Christ come in the flesh'; that means an absolute refusal to dissolve away the concrete actuality of Jesus Christ whether in terms of the idealism of the last century or of the existentialism of this century. The thing we have to convey is not ideas but a concrete relationship to Jesus, attachment to him through his people, through the actual historical community which stems from him. St John speaks of the water and the blood, a visible sacramentally-centred fellowship drawing all men together in the name of Jesus. The name of Jesus is a stumbling-block in a situation such as in India, because it is concrete and refers to a human being who cannot be dissolved away. People find it easier to use the word Christ, because that can be detached from particularity and made into a general idea. But our message is: 'Jesus come in the flesh'. Our relationship with him is through that sacramentally-centred fellowship which stems from him.

If we make this emphasis we must at once be on our guard against petrifying the Church in the social and organisational structures which it develops necessarily from time to time, but which do not have any necessary connection with its essential nature. Frl Cremer has written of this in relation to the situation in Europe, and it is no less relevant to the situation in Asia. How very much of our failure in missionary work is due to the failure to distinguish between that which is essential in the visible form of the Church and that which is merely a thing that our fathers and grandfathers were brought up in! The Willingen conference in

1952 sounded a note in favour of flexibility. I am sorry that the debate following Willingen has centred on the question of the place of institutions such as schools and hospitals, but did not go further and deal with the questions of the forms of Church life itself. There is still a need for debate on fundamental questions regarding the visible forms of Church life and ministry with which the people of God go out to embrace new peoples. There is need to find, e.g., in the situation of an Indian village, that visible form of ministry and congregational life which at the same time shall be authentically one with the whole family of God and yet on the other hand genuinely relevant to the situation there. Too often we have imposed on a new situation the visible forms which we have been brought up with and which were totally unsuited to it.

If my central thesis is true—that what we are witnessing is the drawing together of the human race into that history whose centre is the Cross—then the issue of Christian unity is the most central and critical one for the mission of the Church. Every day that the present fragmentation of Christendom endures makes the Church as it is more and more irrelevant to the task of mission. If our message is Jesus Christ come in the flesh, not just a set of ideas, and if the meaning of what is happening in our time is the gathering up of the human race into history of which the centre is Jesus Christ, then the division of the Church is a flat contradiction of its message at the central point. World community is no longer a matter of the dreams of a few visionaries. It is pressing upon us in its secular form every day. That means that the unity of the Church is a burning issue at the very heart of its world mission, a unity not just in ideas, not just in programme, let me say not just in the kind of togetherness that we are able to enjoy in the Ecumenical Movement and its activities; but a unity in the inner life of liturgy, sacrament and congregational fellowship. If we fail to take that as literally the most crucial issue facing us in relation to the world mission of the Church, how is it possible for us to come to the central point of our witness, i.e. Jesus come in the flesh?

THE MISSION OF THE PEOPLE OF GOD

J. Blauw

INTRODUCTION

WHEN we speak about the Church as 'the people of God in the world' and enquire into the real nature of this Church, we cannot avoid speaking about the *roots* of the Church which are to be found in the Old Testament idea of Israel as the people of the covenant. So the question of the *missionary* nature of the Church, that is, the real relationship between the people of God and the world, cannot be solved until we have investigated the relation between Israel and the nations of the earth. During the whole history of Israel this relation was a problem, and we find in the O.T. various statements concerning the nations. The most fundamental are to be found in the theologically significant first chapters of Genesis (1-11), in which Israel expresses its belief in a very deep and concrete way. To understand the relation between Israel and 'the peoples which do not know Jahveh' this so-called *Urgeschichte* (prehistory) is of the greatest importance. We shall begin our investigation therefore with a short survey of these chapters. After that we shall try to trace out the thoughts expressed there in the following books of the Bible. We shall have of necessity to advance by leaps and bounds. Finally we shall try to draw some theological and practical conclusions.

MAN'S ACTION AND GOD'S REACTION

The stories at the beginning of the Bible seem at first sight to be of a harmless, naïve character. In reality, they belong to the deepest and, theologically speaking, the most far-reaching parts of Holy Scripture. There is an undeniable sadness in these ancient tales. Are they not, in some respects, the story of 'the God who fails' and yet never puts up with his failures? In the beginning, after God had created heaven and earth, the glorious statement is made: 'And God saw everything that he had made and behold it was very good.' Only a short time afterwards, man, the crown of creation, was no longer good. God acknowledged his defeat, but he was not finally cast down: he promised and gave life in spite of the disobedience of man. But the first-born of the mother of all living men became a murderer: the beginning of a corruption which at last caused the Lord to destroy the man whom he had created from the face of the earth: another failure. But even after the flood, God did not give up. He indicated in a rainbow the guarantee that he would never again deal with people in that way. But once again he was disappointed: the reckless men said: 'Go to, let us build us a city and a tower whose top may reach unto heaven and let us make us a name, lest we be scattered abroad upon the face of the whole earth.' Then God took the measures which made of this world such an infinitely troubled world— a Babel of many tongues. Here ends the biblical prehistory (*Urgeschichte*) and it is not a happy ending. Here the tune has been set for the history of our world. It is not we who have invented the perplexities of this fractured world: there is an act of God in it, of that God who always fails. His goodness and grace always meet new deeds of violence and disobedience. Until the story of the Babylonian tower God's answer has always been: more grace, more goodness. But here we seem to be at the end of the story: a scattering and shattering God. What hope for a mankind thus condemned to being scattered?

But this is where the story of Abraham and Israel comes in. The election of Abraham is the *positive* side of God's reaction to man and his recklessness, as the confounding of his language and the scattering abroad upon the face of all the earth was its *negative* side.

In this way the history of Israel, the chosen people, is linked up with the end of the dark and sad prehistory: after the alienation from God, the new covenant with Abraham. In Gen. 12 the same words are used as in Gen. 11. 'Let us make us a name' (11.4). 'I will make thy (Abraham's) name great' (12.2). After the 'scattering abroad' (11.8), the promise 'I will make of thee a great nation' (12.2) 'and in thee shall all families of the earth be blessed' (12.3).

Three conclusions may be drawn from a comparison of the end of the prehistory and the beginning of Israel's history: (a) Both God and man strive for *a name* in this world. As far as they are opposed, God destroys the aims of man. But God will *give* man a name connected with his name. (b) God opposes mankind's search for *unity* as it appears in the way the people who built Babel tried to safeguard this unity, but he promises mankind another unity, a *blessed* unity. Here we are at the roots of the theology of the people of God in the world. The meaning of the election of Israel, i.e. of the people of God, can only be discovered in connection with all families of the earth. The 'people of God' stands from the very beginning against the background of *universal* history. The biblical 'prehistory' is the aetiology of the people of God; and the people of God is from the very beginning directed towards an ecumenical purpose. (c) The history of this world can be characterised as a history of disobedience and recklessness on the side of man, as a history of failure, disappointment and nevertheless perseverance on the side of God.

HISTORY OF ISRAEL

From the beginning the history of Israel is a history of loneliness. Abraham, from the moment he is called by God, has no longer any family or kindred people. Israel is the lonely people which is always faced with the temptation to get rid of this loneliness by identifying itself with other peoples. Nevertheless—Israel exists for all the peoples of the earth. Lonely—in order to prepare the way for the definitive removal of loneliness. During its long history Israel seems to lose sight of this purpose. The people of God is not aware of the fact that by Israel, God makes himself manifest *in the world*, that Israel's experience is intended for all the peoples of the world. Israel fails, and God 'fails' in and with Israel. The first is stressed, especially by Isaiah 40-55; the second is denied by the same prophet, because he knows of the secret of God's redeeming action, even in and through so-called failure.

After the complete failure of Israel, the 'Servant of Jahveh' will come. He represents at one and the same time Israel in its blindness and dumbness, and the Lord 'who builds from his failures his castles of triumph'.

The story of Israel only seems to repeat the story of rebellion from the first eleven chapters of Genesis. But here as there, the 'stubbornness' of God's love for a blessed and united mankind outlasts the stubborn repetition of human sin and repentance.

There is a 'progressive reduction' in the history of revelation: from creation to the many nations (Gen. 1-11); from the nations to Israel; from Israel to a 'remnant'; from the remnant to the one Servant of Jahveh. From the O.T. Servant of Jahveh to Jesus Christ it is only one step. Jesus recognises in the O.T. Servant himself and God himself gives witness to him as the promised Servant (see Isa. 42.1-4, Matt. 3.17). For the last time the history of grace-rebellion-failure-of-God seems to be repeated in the work and crucifixion of Jesus. But in the resurrection of Christ it becomes clear that God has now reached his purpose, the purpose which had been revealed long before to Abraham. A comparison of Gen. 12.3, Isa. 45.22-23 and Phil. 2.9-11 is surprisingly revealing in this respect.

If God through Jesus Christ has definitely overcome human pride and sin, and the frustration which seemed to follow all deeds of grace and goodness in the past—then the moment has also come to fulfil the promise of 'blessing all families of the earth'. Now the 'ecumenical purpose' of God, revealed as his positive answer (Gen. 12) to the disobedience and apostasy of man (Gen. 11), will be realised by the proclamation of Christ throughout the world (Matt. 28.18-20, Mark 16.15-18, Luke 24.46-47, Acts 1.8, Phil. 2.10-11). So the protology is linked up with eschatology. God's final purpose with Jesus Christ as Lord of all is the same as the purpose revealed at the beginning of history. The history of salvation reaches in the death and resurrection of Christ its fulfilment. Therefore Peter can announce the 'last days' at Whitsunday. (Acts 2.17; cf. I Peter 4.7). The new creation is there: Christ, the 'first-born of every creature' (Col. 1.15) and everybody who is in Christ is a new creature: 'old things are passed away; behold, all things are become new' (II Cor. 5.17).

THE PLACE AND FUNCTION OF THE CHURCH

Now, if it is true that God's ultimate purpose has been fulfilled by Christ, that God's 'stubborn' oath (Isa. 45.22-23) has been realised and upheld through Christ (cf. Phil. 2.9-11), that Christ is God's omega identical with his alpha, what does this mean for his Church?

(a) The Church is the gathered, chosen people (*ecclesia*) *who are aware of God's ultimate purpose* and therefore praise him for his deeds and enter into the new relationship which has been given by Christ. The Church is the new *koinonia* between God and man. You remember the naïve story of paradise: with God walking in the garden in the cool of the day, longing for a talk with his earthly friends? The Church is the place where God has anew the opportunity to enter into dialogue with man, because his work is acknowledged and recognised there. There God receives—at last—the right answer to his question: 'Man, where art thou?' Therefore the Church is the visible, unmistakeable token of the conquering and obstinate love of God for man; the place where he is being answered in the right way; a token in the midst of the world, that God has not spoken in vain.

(b) It is only in and through Christ that this right answer can be given by the Church. The Church is only the Church *because* and *if* she *represents* him. *Ubi Christus, ibi ecclesia*—'Where two or three are gathered together in my name, I am in the midst of them'.

As the representative of Christ, the Church has received not only the blessings of God's redeeming grace, the new relationship with him, but also the power of attorney: to proclaim the Kingdom of God and the Lordship of Christ. Christ called his apostles and endowed them with authority as the real representatives and at the same time as the very beginning of the new people of God, which is no longer Israel alone, but all the nations. This apostolic authorisation was unique, but the work of the apostles continues:

the Church carries on their work, both in its ministry and in its laity, heralding the Kingdom of God. A herald proclaims with a given authority news from the King himself. He who has seen Christ (and through him the Father himself: John 14.9) bears witness to him. There is a correlation between *seeing* Christ and *proclaiming* him: the missionary nature of the Church is not an invention of one or another century: it is rooted in Christ himself, who is at the same time the new covenant with God and the new Lord of all. This correlation of Lord and Saviour, Redeemer and King, is constitutive for the Church representing him. This has nothing to do with our obsolete schemes: static-dynamic, active-passive, mobile-immobile, introvert and extrovert, concentration and expansion, cathedral and tent, and the like. The nature of the Church, the missionary nature too, is given in the fact that the Church represents Christ. The more we come to a full knowledge of Christ, the more we acknowledge both the secret of the new communion with God, hidden in him, and the universal claim of his Lordship.

Let us never lose sight of the perspective of the Holy Scripture, which is from the very beginning universal, ecumenical and missionary. A new theology of missions can be nothing other than the result of a new discovery of this perspective.

(c) In these days the question is often raised whether there is a special biblical foundation for *foreign* missions. There is a rather wide-spread conviction that foreign missions have to do with eschatology. Often you find linked together the end of the times and the ends of the earth. Both expressions have in common the New Testament word *eschaton*. That may be one reason why foreign missions, which had to do with the ends of the earth, claimed the end of time too. Another reason is perhaps that famous scheme in western philosophy of 'Time and Space'. A third reason is that missions do indeed have to do with eschatological facts. It must be admitted that it is the missionary societies and those who have considered the theology of missions who discovered the eschatological dimension of our life in this world. In a sense they have thought vicariously, doing what a true Church (representing Christ) ought to do. There was more of the true Church in the non-ecclesiastical missionary societies of the nineteenth century than in most of the official Churches. In our day the missionary nature of the Church as such and the eschatological dimension of the Christian message is acknowledged more and more. This has made it somewhat difficult to find a justification of *foreign* missions by means of eschatology. There is no need for such a special justification. Now we have reached that point in history where we see the Church of Christ present in almost all countries throughout the world, we cannot ignore the Church in other parts of the world even if the task in our own country is overwhelming. We cannot escape the responsibilities given to us in the past and still less the communication and communion which have grown out of foreign mission work. The pattern of foreign missions may change, as it has already changed considerably in several areas, but as long as the Church is aware of a world-wide community in Christ and a world-wide Kingdom of Christ the work will go on. There must be and there will always be a realisation of the world-wide commission conferred on the Church: to fulfil God's ecumenical purpose.

THE CHURCH IN THE WORLD

In the Church's struggle for life, i.e. to maintain its identity as representative of Jesus Christ, and of God's eschatological (and therefore ecumenical) movement in and through him, it always faces three temptations: sacralisation, secularisation and spiritualisation. I do not call them -isms, because I like to stress the action rather than the results.

(*a*) *Sacralisation.* Sacral means 'separated from'. Every religion knows the sacral as a category. The sacral spot is the place marked out, the *templum,* which is elevated above everyday life. As the people of God, representative and token of Christ and the Kingdom of God, the Church cannot exist in the reluctant world without being contested, questioned. As a means of defence the Church can take up the weapon of separatism, of isolation and institutionalism. The first attempt of sacralisation in church history was perhaps Judaism. One may continue with Marcionism, Donatism, and so on. The result is always an *alienation* from the world. Calling upon the name of the Lord never really means alienation from the world, but one can misuse this calling in order to forget, or to escape from the world. The *corpus Christianum* ideology (despite the rich blessings which accompanied it) was a huge and astonishing attempt to reconcile a sacral church with the world around it by sacralising the world too. In sacralisation there is an *anticipation*: it identifies or is tempted to go into the direction of identifying the Church and the Kingdom of God.

The Church is *in* the world but distinguished from the world because it is directed toward God in order to give him thanks and glory as a preliminary fulfilment of the meaning of creation (cf. Rom. 1.21). But *distinguished* is not the same as *isolated*, and this is the heresy of sacralisation. This separatism is usually demonstrated by a one-sided stress upon the ministry at the expense of the Church as a living community, come of age. So sacralisation means paralysing the Church as a witnessing, heralding people.

Now, generally speaking, this danger of sacralisation has been recognised: and we have discovered that fundamentalism and sectarianism are beloved Protestant forms of sacralisation.

(b) As a reaction against, but first of all as a *result* of sacralisation, *secularisation* arises. The irony of history is that by the one-sided stress on the contrast between Church and world, secularisation has a chance in the Church as nowhere else; the more because it can so easily camouflage itself with the robes of office and the attending of church services. If in our day there is a more positive attitude towards secularisation, it is partly because the wrong conception and bad results of sacralisation have been acknowledged, partly because the responsibility for the world, which is Christ's, has been recovered. The stress on the lay apostolate on the one hand, and on the positive significance of secularisation on the other, is a reaction against the magic wand of sacralisation which turns all things into holy gold. If a 'religionless world' means a world which has discovered the irrelevancy of religious and even Christian sacralism, we cannot but be deeply grateful for this world. But it means more. Let us not be so optimistic as to think that rejecting religion automatically means accepting the Gospel or readiness to accept the Gospel. Secularisation cannot do us harm, if we remain faithful to the great Shepherd. Wolves will always appear stronger than sheep, but I do not believe that it is necessary to behave and dress like wolves in order to change the wolves into sheep. In the famous demand for 'identification' we are sometimes perhaps a little bit too much bothered about the clothing of the Church. If people 'outside' like us as men, as human beings, they will like us to speak as honestly as possible about our real aims and purposes as ambassadors of Christ. Having this in mind we can whole-heartedly agree with those who stress the need of being this-worldly in our concern for people, rather than other-worldly. God has loved this world as it is, in all its sinfulness and alienation from him. God intends to purify his creatures rather than sacralise them. We need a sharp distinction between sacred and sacral. People who intend a sacred Church often give the impression of aiming at a sacral Church; people whose object is a Church open to the world express themselves sometimes in such a way that they are suspected of being secularists. We have not yet entirely overcome our Babel confusion.

(c) The third temptation of the Church in the struggle for its identity as representative of Christ is *spiritualisation*. It shares with secularisation the horror of a sacral Church (especially institutionalism); it shares with sacralisation the stress laid on isolation from the world. But it denies the world; it has written the world off, as 'going to perish'. It is only interested in a spiritual understanding of the Gospel; it is a denial of incarnation. Mysticism knows little about Jesus Christ and his kingship, and more about religious experience. From the days of the gnostics until now the Church is weakened by the influence of these spiritualists. Usually they are so attached to the status quo in politics, society and church life that they are the biggest stumbling blocks on the way to a real Christianisation of life (in which they do not believe, of course). They are in fact the most dangerous secularists, because they deny all relationship between God and his world; and often behave as sacralists because they are so isolated that they do not welcome anybody who does not belong to their company.

THE MISSIONARY CHURCH IN THE WORLD

The heresies mentioned above endanger the missionary as well as the Church in its home-life. To be mission-minded, and even to be a missionary, is no guarantee in itself. We have always to struggle for our identity as Christ's disciples, representatives, servants. Only the guidance of the Holy Spirit prevents us from becoming sacralists in a sentimental attachment to old patterns of missions or a fanatic propaganda for new ones. We can become secularists in making a gospel out of our relevancy, our timeliness, instead of making *the* Gospel relevant. The Gospel will always be irrelevant for all people of all times, because 'it is not after man' (Gal. 1.11). 'For if I yet pleased men I should not be the servant of Christ' (Gal. 1.10). We may become spiritualists in escaping the responsibility to preach the Gospel in an articulate way, for people of our time. Always we have to look at Christ as the Head of the Church and the King of the world. The Church will only be capable of remaining his Church in a new and continually renewed community with God (sacred, not sacral); looking toward the world (secular, not secularist); in a life distinguished, but not isolated, from the world (spiritual, not spiritualist). There is an interdependency in these three phrases: *in* the world, *for* the world, and not *of* the world. But it is an over-simplification to preserve one of these aspects for special concern. The missionary nature of the Church can only be maintained by a missionary spirit. Separating one from the other will always obscure the real nature of the Church, as it has been so often obscured in history.

Christ is not divided. He is at the same time Redeemer and Judge, Saviour and King, Shepherd and Mediator, Servant and Lord. It is not a simple thing to represent him. 'But we all, with open face beholding as in a glass the glory of the Lord, are changed into the same image from glory to glory, as by the Spirit of the Lord' (II Cor. 3.18).

THE MARKS OF AN EVANGELISING
CHURCH

EXPERIENCES AND PERSPECTIVES DRAWN FROM
THE RENEWAL OF THE CHURCHES IN THE WEST

Hans-Ruedi Weber

I. THE CHURCH'S MISSION: TO WORK WITH CHRIST
IN GIVING SERVICE IN THE WORLD

WHEN rain comes in Uganda after the long drought, the congregation at Mukono gathers for a service of thanksgiving. The rain-water, the soil, the young plants and the agricultural implements are brought to the altar, and finally all the Christians offer themselves to God as thank offerings.

From the modern industrial world of the West one could look almost with envy at this congregation in whose Sunday and everyday life God is still so real, just because they are so directly dependent upon the Creator and Sustainer of this world. We pavement-dwellers have almost completely lost touch with the soil; we are entirely dependent upon the hectic rhythm of the machine; we are no longer part of the rhythm of nature.

But God is also the centre of the modern industrial world. In one Anglican Church in an industrial district on 'Labour Sunday' it was not only the bread and the wine which were laid on the altar; a miner brought a piece of coal, an engineer a machine-part, and a textile-worker a piece of cloth.

This is the liturgical portrayal of what is really happening in the renewal of the Church in the West. We are looking for a new, biblical view of the right relation between Sunday and weekday, worship and work, the sacred and the secular, the Church and the world.

If one talks with the pioneers of Church renewal—either in

religious North America or in France (which is completely secu-larised), whether it be with industrial chaplains who are working outside the traditional structure of the Churches or with pastors and laymen who are working for the renewal of the Church within the existing structure—one discovers a growing consensus. The books and initiatives of Dietrich Bonhoeffer, Hendrik Kraemer, Martin Buber, E. Rosenstock-Huessy and others are often men-tioned in this connection. Many of these pioneers acknowledge their debt to the theology of Karl Barth, who has stimulated them and given them his comments; and they are all striving to build up an experimental apostolic theology.

In this the question of the relation between Church and world is of decisive importance. At the time of the *corpus Christianum* the influence of the Church was felt in every sphere of life. But since then, owing to the process of secularisation, more and more of the secular spheres have become independent of the Church. This means that the Church has been forced back into a ghetto, in which it is restricted to one sector only of human life: the sphere of religion. Whether this religious sphere is large (as in the present religious boom in North America) or growing smaller and smaller (as in many countries in Europe, so that one can speak with Bonhoeffer of a 'world without religion'), is a secondary question.

The new outlook begins by taking Christ's Lordship over *the Church and the world* seriously. This puts an end to the laments about the godless process of secularisation. It is recognised as one of God's ironic ways of recalling the Church to be really the Church. There is one form of secularising the world which is genuine and blessed, and secularism is 'Christian heresy' rather than neo-paganism. That is why we must welcome the fact that the world has 'reached maturity'—even if our approval is not entirely without reservation.

It is just in its normal minority-position that the Church recog-nises itself to be the Body of which Christ is the Head, who is at the same time the Head of all things (Eph. 1.20-3).

'In the "world which has reached maturity" the Church will

renounce any claim to clerical domination and any attempt to "churchify" the world—not because it is forced to do so, but because it realises the true nature of its ministry to the world. The new attitude of the Church to the world will then have to be one of service' (H. D. Wendland). The Church's mission thus consists in *being* the Body of Christ, of serving with Christ.

One important form of this service is fulfilled when the Christians in the world are 'contagiously human'. For on this also a consensus is growing, that being human means bearing one another's burdens, and that it is precisely this which is the essence of being a Christian. Christians cannot be contagiously human in daily life unless they bear the burdens of others in the fellowship of the communion of saints with their Lord.

We have thus mentioned two essential characteristics of the missionary congregation; for this 'serving with Christ' (*diakonia*) and this 'togetherness in Christ' (*koinonia*) are the basic elements of the Church's message. This does not mean that the word is neglected. Rather it gains the proper sounding board, it finds its true setting, so that it can be spoken with authority and decisiveness. The true dialogue with the world begins. It must first be the communion of saints to which the world puts its questions. And then the members of that communion may account with words for the hope that is in them (I Peter 3.15).

How can a spontaneously missionary Church of this kind be equipped, and what are its structural forms?

2. THE EQUIPPING OF A MISSIONARY CONGREGATION

1. Something must first be said about *the right and wrong relationships between the so-called 'ministry' and the so-called 'laity'*.

No one will deny that the real 'minister' is Christ. He is the pastor, the teacher, the prophet, the evangelist, the apostle, the healer, and so with all the other offices. But if one then asks, who is sharing in Christ's service (Latin *ministerium*) in the world in the interval between his ascension and his return, the whole Church replies in practice: the official clergy, the 'ministry', as pastors are called in many Churches.

We cannot speak in this way today without having a bad conscience. For one of the main discoveries made during the renewal of the Church in the West is precisely the rediscovery of the laity. 'The laity are the frozen capital of the Church' was one of Professor H. Kraemer's slogans, when he went from congregation to congregation at the beginning of the renewal of the Church in Holland, and roused the pastors and the laity to co-operate in rebuilding parish life. Today lay work has become the fashion. Everywhere the laity are being 'mobilised'; everywhere 'teams of helpers' are springing up.

Nevertheless, people still cling to the old ways of thought. Who is helping whom? Even today the team of helpers is usually not much more than a team of 'pastor's assistants'. The laity help the 'minister' (the pastor or star-evangelist) to carry out his *ministerium*. Clericalism remains unbroken.

But the biblical view of the true relationship between the functions of the 'office-holders' and the 'laity' is completely different. The help must be given in the opposite direction: Christ made 'some prophets, some evangelists, and some pastors and teachers, for the perfecting of the saints, for the work of the ministry' (Eph. 4.11-12). It is not primarily the 'office-bearers' but the 'saints', the 'laity', the congregation as a whole, whom Christ calls to co-operate with him in his work of service (Greek *diakonia*, Latin *ministerium*). The 'ministry' therefore consists not of the office-holders but of the congregation. And in order that the congregations may be equipped to carry out this service, Christ has given the Church special people endowed with the gifts of the spirit or *charismata*.

The true function of the latter is not to do 'the work of service'. That service cannot be delegated by the congregation to 'office-holders'. The special function of those with spiritual gifts is the training of the saints. Help must be given by the pastor to the group of helpers, so that they may arrive at that 'relationship of service' between Church and world. One might express this (in somewhat exaggerated terms) in the old symbol of the 'Church militant'; the soldiers at the front are the laity, whose daily lives bring them up against the points where Christ wants to carry out his service as prophet, priest and king. The office-holders are the food-orderlies, the kitchen police (and perhaps also to some extent the officers and general staff). But as we shall see, this analogy will have to be clarified and extended, in order to make the real situation clear.

In Ephesians 4.11ff. the training of the apostles and evangelists is exactly the same as that of the prophets, pastors and teachers. Their primary task is not to evangelise the congregation, but to rouse them and equip them for *their* task of evangelism. The office of apostle was a unique office which no longer exists today; it is questionable, also, whether the service of evangelists described in Ephesians 4 may be compared with the evangelistic work known to us today. Nevertheless far-reaching conclusions may be drawn from Ephesians 4, not only concerning the work of pastors but also concerning the work of evangelists and missionaries; the research undertaken some decades ago by the missionary scholar, Roland Allen, has become timely again at this point.

2. The passage referred to from the Epistle to the Ephesians takes us still further. We can no longer speak of a pastor or evangelist responsible for all the work of equipping the saints, but are instead made aware of the *diversity of those possessing spiritual gifts*.

This diversity of the spiritually gifted has always existed, even where Church usage or established canonical law makes for the one-man system. Fortunately the power of the Holy Spirit is greater than Church usage and canonical law. During the renewal of the Churches in the West, too, it has brought into being new forms of service within the Church. The fact that the service of these new *charismata* is not yet recognised by most ecclesiastical governing bodies and canonical laws (many of them are in fact pastors 'on leave of absence from Church duties'!), is simply a sign that the Churches in question are sick, and does not call in question at the outset the genuineness of the service.

Whence comes this diversity among those with spiritual gifts? It seems that in the early Christian communities it was not the practice first to see what services were required for the equipping of the saints, and then to be on the lookout for men and women qualified to perform those services. We may rather suppose that the congregations were able through their powers of discernment to recognise the men and women with spiritual gifts whom Christ had given them, and called them to the perfecting of the saints. How many such men and women may be going unrecognised in our congregations! Because we in our blindness fail to recognise those with such gifts and take them into service, their gifts wither away, or else they are led to carry out their service in sects.

We can be certain that Christ always gives to his Church the men and women of gifts that it needs in a given situation and at a given time in world history. Indeed, we can see how throughout the history of the Church congregations have received the people thus qualified to equip them for their service. And this is still true today: for instance, in the hectic rhythm of modern life, hardly anything is more urgently needed than quiet and reflection; it is at this very time that Christ has given us brotherhoods and sisterhoods which are performing the service of retreat to equip the saints for their service in the world. The Church and the world today need meeting-places, places where discussion can go on; Christ has given us men and women with spiritual gifts who are performing this service of training by running conference centres, evangelical academies, and the like.

When we give the Spirit scope, then we may well become dismayed at the dynamic force of this Spirit. Indeed, there actually is a great movement of the Spirit in our day, which has been called 'the new, third branch of the Christian faith', alongside Catholicism and Protestantism. In South America the majority of non-Roman Catholic Christians belong to such 'Pentecostal sects', and in other continents too similar movements of the Spirit are developing an explosive missionary impetus.

It is therefore good for us to remember that 'God is not a God of confusion, but of peace', who seeks to ensure peace and unity in the Church. Should not therefore all those recognised and taken into service by the Church as having spiritual gifts be ordained? The diversity of the *charismata* must be an ordered diversity.

3. Let us now pass on and try to imagine the *picture of a Church* in which those with spiritual gifts see as their main task 'the perfecting of the saints for the work of the ministry', in which there is truly a diversity of spiritually gifted, and in which all members of that company are ordained (that is to say where it is not the case that non-ordained members of a 'team of helpers' are assisting one ordained man).

First of all it must be said that the dividing line between 'office-holders' and 'laymen' is becoming fluid. When the distinction is made, it is primarily a differentiation of the functions and not so much a differentiation of persons. That ought to find expression above all in worship: worship is a festival of the entire congregation, in which each individual has something to contribute to the edifying of the brethren (I Cor. 14.26). It is precisely this taking part in the mutual edification of the congregation that is the best preparation for the role of 'salt of the earth' which that congregation is called upon to play on being sent out into the world at the end of the service.

For the 'official clergy' this view raises the following questions, which appear unusual and revolutionary only to our 'normal' Church way of thinking, but are in reality the simple biblical questions addressed to our abnormal ecclesiastical life.

Is it absolutely necessary that the spiritually gifted who are recognised and ordained for service by the congregation should be 'professional Christians', 'completely official Christians'? Paul was a tentmaker, and we know that many of the clergy, even the bishops, during the first four or five centuries were not professional holders of their office. Particularly in our day it will probably be necessary again and again for individual possessors of spiritual gifts to be left completely free to carry out their work of training. But generally speaking, is it not in fact desirable that someone with 'official' duties should also have 'lay' duties to carry out, and is not the best preparation for fulfilling 'lay' functions precisely participation in the functions of the 'official clergy-man'? In areas where there are young Churches, everywhere where there is a Church in a minority position, and also, above all in the Churches in Communist countries, this question of non-professional 'office-holders' is an extremely urgent one at the present time. It should come to us and we should deal with it, however, not merely as a practical question, but as a funda-mental theological one. It may be that with the present scarcity of pastors God is taking this way of helping us to a more biblical conception of the role of the official clergyman.

Is there no alternative but for the spiritually gifted who have been recognised and ordained by the congregation to exercise the function of 'official clergyman' all their life long? According to the pastoral epistles, the position was that the 'office-holder' should be someone 'that ruleth well his own house, having his children in subjection with all gravity': they were thus for the most part persons of middle age, who had already proved their worth as 'laymen'. But what a need there is for some theologians to turn journalists and try in that capacity to see and report on everyday happenings in the light of the Gospel, instead of always complaining about the shallowness of journalists. And what a source of blessing it might be if some engineers, or workers, or the like, with their knowledge of the modern world of industry, were to become pastors, instead of always complaining about the clergy being away up in the clouds.

Is there no alternative but for all the spiritually gifted who are recognised and ordained by the Church to have studied theology? The service rendered by the theologians is of decisive import-ance. We need better theologians (I am not in favour of doing away with the study of Hebrew!). But is it essential for pastors to be theologians? The way in which theological studies and preparation for the role of 'office-holder' have come to be linked, almost indissolubly, in the western Churches is now having serious consequences in the young Churches of Asia and Africa. It is also a handicap in many respects to church life in the West. We have to think here not only of the barrier which an academic training may create between pastor and congregation. Even more important: the absence of any distinction between theological studies and training for the role of 'office-holder' has led to the unfortunate and widespread misconception that theology is something only for 'office-holders'. In reality, however, theological thinking and judgment are of the utmost importance precisely for the 'laity'. In the work of parents, politicians, technicians, etc., theologically important decisions must be made every day. But are 'laymen' theologically equipped to make such decisions in a responsible manner? What is the right theological training for the 'layman's' role? This concern about the adults' catechism, about the constant progress from infancy to adulthood (Eph. 4.12-16) is highly important: we do not even know the ABC of this theological training for the layman today; for the 'layman's theology' will surely be quite a different theology, in its mode of expression and form, from the 'theology of the theologians'.

Is there no alternative but for all the spiritually gifted who are recognised and ordained by the Church to be bound to a particular place, to a local congregation? In the early Church there were many mobile *charismata*. Does not our modern, highly mobile society, with its many strata, also call for the creation of many more mobile and regional services of preparation? But that brings us right into questions of Church structure.

3. THE STRUCTURE OF AN EVANGELISING CHURCH

1. It should first be emphasised that *the Church* lives *not only in assembly, but in dispersion too*. In the time between Christ's ascension and his second coming the Church of Christ has two forms of existence: that of the *ecclesia*, the assembly, and that of the *diaspora*, the dispersion. Pastors whose service is given mainly in the assemblies of God's people are always in danger of regarding the Church much too exclusively from the standpoint of the assembly. This narrow conception of the Church has also had an effect on the whole of ecclesiastical thought regarding the laity: those who spend most time in Church premises and organisations are looked upon as 'active laymen'. The true role of the

laity in the Church is apparent not in its *ecclesia* form, however, but in the *diaspora*. When Peter and James write to the Church which is 'scattered abroad', they are thus indicating more than merely a state of affairs of sociological import: the 'normal' form of existence of the Church is in our 'interim time' the *diaspora*. No doubt the Church can and should meet again and again, become visible and thereby, acting vicariously for the whole world, show forth before the time God's people of the latter days and be with its Head (Rev. 7.9ff.). Without *this* form of divine service, the Church living in dispersion would never be able in the everyday life of this world to arrive at that other form of divine service in which we must present our whole lives as 'a living sacrifice, holy, acceptable unto God' (Rom. 12.1-2). If that is to be done then the coming together of the Church must be effected with a view to its future dispersion at the beginning of this paper, as in the two services of worship described. What happens in the small circle of the congregation gathered for worship must also be a preparation for the role of 'salt of the earth' which is that of the larger, concentric circle of the Church in dispersion in everyday life. We come together in order to go apart. That is why the blessing at the end of the meeting for worship is, with the celebration of Communion, the most sacred moment: it is an echo of the great missionary command of Matthew 28 and hence the establishing of the Church in its 'layman's' role in the world.

Are the present forms and structures for gathering the Church adapted in this way with a view to preparing the congregation for service in the world? Or is it not rather the case that much of what occurs at divine service, in church organisations and other forms of ecclesiastical assembly is more apt to turn the congregation away from its work in the world and make it incapable of doing that work? Sociological investigations into ecclesiastical structural forms in order to find an answer to these questions can become for the congregation a means to self-knowledge and realistic self-criticism (this does not mean that the Church has any lesson to learn from sociology as to its own true nature and its mission in the world, or need be thereby led into error regarding its belief in the kingship of Christ, which can cut across even sociological laws).

2. For some years now *studies on ecclesiastical structures* have been in progress, particularly in the Roman Catholic Church in France. They indicate first of all how the traditional parish is living as it were in a ghetto. Historical studies reveal how the structural form of the Roman Catholic Church has been constantly changing down the centuries. The present-day parish structure is almost entirely determined by the dimension of place, whereas today the dimension of work, which in most cases no longer coincides with the dimension of place, is the deciding factor. Thus it is almost impossible for the Roman Catholic Church in its traditional structure to 'perfect the saints for the work of the ministry'. It is therefore necessary to supplement the parish with 'movements', for example by means of the specialised Catholic Action or the work of the so-called 'secular institutions'. In this connection special reference is made to the significance of small cells and of the *communautés de quartiers*.

Protestant investigations on the same subject have produced quite similar findings. Thus for instance the Dutch theologian H. Hoekendijk has indicated how in German missionary studies and practice the concept 'nation' came more and more to be regarded and theologically coloured as a special order of creation. As in so many instances, the Church here consecrated a social structural form and through that 'ethnopathetic attitude' has become blind to the concrete environment of the human being and the structural changes of the modern world. In the face of this 'ordinology' Hoekendijk advocates an 'ecology' that addresses itself to the human being in whatever may be his concrete *oikos* (=house, concrete social milieu). Instead of making the existing, established local congregation the focal point of a missionary Church, the human being in his *oikos* must become the focal point. But this must mean not that everything will be brought into and put into line with the existing local congregation. The Church must grow through house congregations, which come into being in the concrete 'houses' of the community.

Such studies can help us to find answers to the questions which arise for the Church in the face of the extremely mobile society of the modern industrial world with its many different strata. The Church cannot possibly cling to archaic structural forms, even consecrated ones. At the same time, however, she must not adapt herself to the world to such an extent that she loses her true character (as has been frequently the case in liberal Protestantism), nor must she become so divided in the multiplicity of strata and in mobility that she completely lose her unity and continuity, that is to say her catholicity and her apostolic character (as is often the case in the Pentecostal Churches and all sects). But then what kind of structure is the appropriate one for a Church that is in keeping with the ordinances of revelation and yet at the same time takes into account the many strata and the mobility of modern society?

In seeking an answer to that question, it is important to recognise that the exclusive claim often made by the local congregation to be the Church of Christ is heretical. Every heresy is something of truth that wrongly puts forward an exclusive claim. It is true that the geographically determined local congregation is and will remain one of the most important structural forms of the Church. But there are others besides, that are equally genuine and important structural forms of the Church.

3. In the New Testament the same term for the assembled church—*ecclesia*—is used for a house congregation (like the church which came into being in the house of Philemon), for a local congregation (like the church in Corinth), for a regional Church (like the Church in Asia Minor), and for the world-wide Church of all countries and peoples and periods. It is always the same reality that is being referred to. The primary and the sole decisive constituent factor of the Church is after all Christ, and he is not tied down to either large or small numbers.

This use of the term *ecclesia* on so many different levels points us to *some important basic forms of the structure of an evangelising Church*.

Perhaps the most important is the rediscovery of the New Testament house church. The early Christian Church lived and grew essentially in and through house congregations. Whereas the *oikos*, the concrete social milieu, mostly consisted at that time of the patriarchal family of antiquity, today the 'house' can be a neighbourhood in the place dimension or group in the work dimension (university church, factory church, and so on). What is essential is that the house church should be a small group within an existing or still-to-be-created observable community of life or work. Thus what is meant is neither the traditional women's, men's or youth group within a local church, nor the already existing house Bible groups and church neighbourhood evenings (although the latter can be preliminary steps towards the house church). The house church is rather a community in the full sense of the word. The four constituent factors of the Church that are named in Acts 2.42—the continuing in the apostles' doctrine, the fellowship, the breaking of bread, and prayer—can and should be given full expression in the gatherings of the house church. As the individual of today lives in more than one *oikos* there is nothing unusual in his being a member of more than one house church.

It is just when the house church is a community in the full sense of the word that its members will desire a more comprehensive manifestation of the fellowship of the saints. Wherever and whenever it is possible for them to do so, they will meet with the members of other house churches. Today we know three types of such a church structure, reaching out beyond the house church: the 'parishes' which are typical of the Roman Catholic Church, the Orthodox and European Protestant established and national Churches, which mostly coincide with a geographically determined area of political administration; the 'congregations' typical of the European Free Churches and the denominations of America, which bring men together out of various administrative areas after the manner of a club; and lastly the 'Christian colonies' which are typical of some mission fields and young Churches in Asia and Africa, and in which the Christians are withdrawn from their natural social milieu and gathered together in 'Christian villages'. All these three types of the more comprehensive structural form of the Church must change. For these local churches should surely be an organic whole composed of various house churches working and living together, and not merely a sum of individual believers or church associations. At the level of the local church the building up of the Church therefore means essentially the developing of various house churches, which would then probably bring about the reaction of a possible change in parish boundaries, a reintegration of the congregations and the disbanding of the colonies.

Beyond the house churches and the local churches the Church of Christ must also become a complete reality in a wider geographical field. Today in particular, when important sectors of the world's life are proceeding not at parochial, but at regional level, the regional Church is of the utmost importance. It is therefore desirable that this regional Church should occasionally become visible in a church assembly. A regional church centre or evangelical academy and a regional house of retreat can contribute much to the building of the Church and to its life as a Church at the regional level. Regional services 'for the perfecting of the saints for the work of the ministry' are just as important as the service of the office-holder in the local church. There must therefore be more mobile, regional office-holders, and not only bishops and chairmen of synods.

More and more people have such an unsettled life, because of their work or for other reasons, that they can no longer be full members of a purely local parish, congregation or colony and a regional Church, but at most still belong to a house church. Many employees of land, sea and air transport undertakings, businessmen, politicians, employees of international organisations and the unfortunately ever-growing number of refugees come into this category. For them a very old structure of community existence is becoming important: the brotherhood church. There have been times in which the Church of Christ existed largely as a brotherhood church (e.g. in Celtic Christendom). And there are today many indications that this fraternal form of church structure is again becoming significant.

Whether the Church of Christ should take form as a national and radical power to the extent that it does today appears to me questionable. At all events the structural forms hitherto discussed, on the one hand, and the ecumenical structural form of the Church which is still to be dealt with, on the other, are of greater significance today.

As we acknowledge in the confession of faith, there is one universal, apostolic and catholic Church, that is to say the reality of a world-wide community of all lands and peoples and ages. The consciousness of membership in this one world-wide community was very strong in the early Church. In the Ecumenical Movement we are now learning again to recognise and experience something of this reality. It is not a matter here of organising an enormous world Church; but of manifesting the world-wide community. This probably becomes most apparent in the work of Inter-Church Aid and the Refugee Service, where something of the world-wide *koinonia* and *diakonia* comes into view. But this world-wide Church is also being built by prayer of intercession, by listening together to the teachings of the apostles, and we long for the day when we shall also be able to 'break bread' together.

4. The structures of an evangelising Church lie *in the field of tension between the normal process of institutionalisation and the dynamic drive of the Holy Spirit.*

We do well to take seriously the sociological law of institutionalisation. Even the best structural form can be attacked by sclerosis. Church institutions and movements which only a century ago were extremely promising tokens of renewal—like the homes for deaconesses, for instance—are now in a state of crisis. All the innovations which we now rightly regard as signs of renewal in the Church may also be attacked in a few decades by the process of institutionalisation.

Therefore perhaps the most important thing that an evangelising Church has to learn is how to die. The sacraments of the

Church are sacraments of death: at baptism we are 'drowned' (to use Luther's expression), and at communion the Body of Christ is broken. The Church which professes these sacraments, however, has not yet learned sufficiently not to hold fast to its own life, and to let die all that does not serve participation in the ministry of Christ in the world.

Fortunately God sees to it that again and again the storms of world history turn church façades into ruins. But that same God often infuses new life into old forms through his Spirit. He gives us new *charismata*, and with them new structures for the service of the Church in the world.

MISSION IN EAST AND WEST

Charles C. West

THE reader who has followed us thus far may well have reason
to wonder whether there is a common thread which runs through
the chapters which have preceded and the conference which gave
rise to them. Is there one direction in the radically different inter-
pretations of the world given us by Frl Cremer in Germany,
Mr Sihombing in Indonesia and Dr van Leeuwen in the Islamic
world? Do we begin to see the outlines of a Church which would
be missionary in this world? Without doing violence to the concrete diversity of all that has been written so far, this chapter
would like to attempt an answer to these questions.

THE WORLD

The reader of Frl Cremer and Mr Sihombing will perceive
a paradox, which expressed itself the more vividly in the international group which first heard these addresses. From Germany,
shattered by war and defeat but nevertheless remarkably intact
and stable, the deepest experience comes of shattered human
community, of lost hopes and spoiled human relations. Voices
from Sweden, France, Britain and the USA bore witness that
what Frl Cremer was describing was not unique, but the process
of inner decay at work in all these lands, even though covered
by a remarkable revival of religion in America, the noise of batt-
ling ideologies in France, or the discipline of custom in Britain.
In all these countries there seems to have been a break through,
not always fully conscious, into a truly religionless condition which
acts as a solvent on all society and culture. On the other hand,
it is from a land in rapid social change, where ancient societies
are being shattered and men uprooted, that one hears the note
of confidence in the future, of national and social aspiration and

loyalty. Here too the testimony of other Asians strengthened that of Mr Sihombing. There were differences of emphasis. Some had more of a sense of broken tradition than others. But for all, national and cultural community was a reality pregnant with hope, whatever the present chaos. The differing Christian insights which come out of these different experiences give rise to one of the most basic dialogues in the Church today.

Dr van Leeuwen's analysis of Islam's attempts to control its modern environment with an ancient religion brings a third element into the picture. It is in one sense a case study, but in another sense symbolic of the efforts of all religions today. Islam is not alone in propagating and enforcing dogmas in which its leaders themselves no longer believe, for the sake of social cohesion and order. One is reminded of the Soviet Union, but equally of somewhat milder attempts to use the Christian religion in this way, in Germany and the United States. Muslim fundamentalism and the lack of any discernible renewal of the inner life pose questions about other religions as well. Is it not a natural process for a religion which sets out to order modern society into its system, to become at once totalitarian and hypocritical in its pretensions, while its inner substance of faith and devotion atrophies? Have we Christians been any more successful in controlling the modern technological civilisation which sprang out of Christendom itself than have the Muslims in controlling the cultural and social influences of an alien west? Is Muslim fundamentalism a mirror of our religious failure also to understand what God is doing with the world?

This brings us to the central questions of our theological understanding of the world. We shall divide them into four:

(a) Is there a secular realm which Christians are called upon to defend from all ideological encroachments, religious or otherwise, Christian or pagan? Should we, as Christian evangelists, rejoice in and further the process whereby religion is more and more losing its influence and appeal? Should we find in religionless, post-war Germany a more fruitful field for Christian evangelism than, for example, an America in the grip of a religious revival which hides from its own emptiness? Should we side in India, Indonesia and elsewhere with the secularists against those who seek to maintain a religious foundation for the state and the culture? Concretely, should the Christian affirm the first principle of the Indonesian *Pantjasila*—respect for Almighty Godhead —as a foundation of the state, with all the features of a Muslim interpretation which this involves? If so, should Christians draw therefrom the implication that they must co-operate with the Muslims in developing a certain common theistic philosophy and ethic for education and politics? Or is reference to the Almighty Godhead out of place in a constitution? If so, what spiritual cohesion for society can Christians propose and support?

A German study group has put this question with special force: 'Is there a really secular realm which is free from religion and from religious ideology, where the Christian can work without fear of being threatened and overcome by demonic powers? If so, how far does it go? There are areas into which the Christian may not enter, or, if he does, then only with a clear denial of them, as for instance the Communist Party in East Germany; on the other side, there can be a co-operation between Christians and Communists over against a state which bears some of the characteristics of Revelation 13, as, for example, in the time of Nazism in Germany or perhaps in Indonesia, where the opponent is the Muslim Party's attempt to create a religious state. But it is easier for the Christian to say 'no' together with non-Christians over against some power which threatens them both, than it is to join with non-Christians in the common work for social development, because for each the value of that which is being built, its place in the total framework of value, is different. Here is one point where the question, how far common action in the secular realm is possible, becomes acute.'

There is a covert ideology in secularism itself, which seeks to escape that real history which can only be understood in relation to God's command and gift. 'Yet secularism also is a judgment on our temptation to be other-worldly, to separate body and soul, mind and spirit, Church and world. God, in Christ's incarnation, suffering, resurrection and ascension, declares that we cannot be with him unless we take this world seriously as a place for his creative and redemptive action.'

It is clear that the secular realm, so far as it exists, is a precarious and threatened field of human life. One may well question, as the German group has done, whether it is not always beset by one ideology or another. One certainly may not understand it apart from the claim of Jesus Christ to be its Lord in every part. It is in no sense a realm with its own laws and ethics. Yet, on the other side, we learned by our discussion that there is an inner contradiction in every religious attempt to order this secular world into a particular system of faith and thought. So far as the Christian is called upon to defend the secular and to oppose religion, even Christian religion, this calling comes directly from his confidence that the secular world is, in fact, in the hands of a redeeming God, that he is at work in and through our relations with our neighbours, our relative decisions as to the best possible state, community form, development of industry, use of natural resources, educational system and the like.

(b) How, then, do we participate with non-Christians in this world, and where do we find the issue where our participation bears a distinctive Christian witness? This leads to the further question, how can we find true partnership as Christians, despite the very different worlds to which we minister in this task? The problem with which we are confronted in this situation is the sharing of experiences between those who have known real spiritual insecurity, and those who have not. It is the problem of creating personal bonds between Christians whose faith is naturally and institutionally expressed through the culture of their country and those for whom Christian faith involves a radical break, with all the insecurities that brings. It is the problem of concentrating the resources of the Church of Jesus Christ on helping those Christians who must make culture-forming decisions in lands like those of Asia and Africa on the one hand, and those who face different problems of restoring personal relations in a land like Germany, on the other. It may involve participating in movements based on false or ideological hopes, in the confidence that, nevertheless, some good purpose will be served, as, for example, the political parties and economic movements of India. It may involve radical rejection of such movements in order to be a companion to people who are basically suspicious and hopeless. Or it may involve simply taking part realistically in the process of community-building, step by step.

In all of this the question of the form of Church life is posed. The traditional realm of inner life, whose destruction Frl Cremer describes in Germany, has been lost in other countries as well. New communities are being formed which correspond to the realities of industrialised cities, or which express the needs of people who have been torn from their traditional family and communal ties. What does this imply for the structure of the congregation, for the times when it meets and for the form of its activity?

(c) Bishop Newbigin, in his contribution to this volume, presents the thesis that the world is being more and more caught up into that history whose centre is the Cross and whose end is the final judgment and mercy of God. The world, therefore, may look differently upon its own condition, in different places. But the crisis with which it is confronted and the historical decision demanded of it are fundamentally the same. For the Christian, cultural pluralism is a temporary and relative matter. The answer to the claim of Hindus to express the religious genius of India, of Buddhists that of Ceylon and Burma, of Muslims that of Indonesia and the Middle East, or for that matter the claim of Protestantism to express the culture of the United States and of Roman Catholicism that of Spain and Italy, is that we are confronted with one God and caught up into the history which he has made and in which he has given his Son for our redemption, and which he will bring to judgment and fulfilment in his time. This is an article of our faith. Our analysis of the world around us is affected by it. The contradictions we find in Islam's attempts to integrate societies where it is dominant, the beginnings which we see of a crisis in Hinduism, are signs of this fact. There is not one history for the East and another for the West. The forces of nationalism, Communism, industrialisation, and even world alliances one against the other, demonstrate both the increasing oneness of our history and the critical nature of the decisions it demands of us. This does not mean that western culture possesses an inherent superiority because it has lived longer in the knowledge of this history. Basically, East and West are confronted with the same crisis. The lands which have been Christian and have become secularised may require a different evangelistic approach, especially because they are more inclined to identify the history of salvation with their own conservative or revolutionary philosophies, but they, no less than those lands which are beginning to learn for the first time the meaning of this history, are being called upon to face the same decisions which are everywhere demanded of us.

(d) This means that the history of the world is, for the Christian, the scene of a conflict and a hope. Bishop Newbigin has put this dialectic so completely that we do not need to repeat it here. He has left us, however, with the question, how this works out in practice. As Christians, we know that we are called into the world to serve the world in the name of the crucified Christ, because we do not depend upon the world for our hope or our calling. How do we then remain realistic about all human plans and hopes, without separating ourselves into a little group of people who know better than those who are working to realise these plans and hopes? How can we warn enthusiastic social planners, land-reformers and revolutionaries about the danger of God's judgment, without ourselves becoming Pharisees? The question can be otherwise stated. If we are called to plunge ourselves into all the nationalist and reform movements which are now at work in Asia and Africa, how can we as Christians demonstrate that we are truly revolutionary, unflagging in our creative effort, while we relativise and question the false hopes which all these movements contain? Three examples from India make this dilemma concrete. (1) Christ is at work also in movements which are not Christian, but where we see foundations of justice and love, as for example in the land-gift movement, led by the Indian

saint and follower of Gandhi, Vinoba Bhave. How can we bear
witness to what Christ is doing there, distinguishing it at the
same time from the idealistic illusions of the movement? (2) On
the other hand, Antichrist is at work in the intrinsically totalitarian claims which a welfare state such as India makes in a non-
Christian society. How can we resist these without resisting at
the same time that which this state accomplishes toward justice
and order? (3) In the field of education, united syncretism presents its sharpest challenge, inviting Christians to participate, but
demanding a common act of worship. Where are the points at
which the Christian must make a compromise, even with a false
ideology, in order to make his concrete witness where men
actually live and work, and what are the limits of this compromise?

This is the dialectic of the revolutionary optimism of Asia and
Africa. When we are confronted with the cynics and egoists of
the western world, enclosed in concern for their own security
and private interests, how do we demonstrate to them what hope
for the world might mean? What form might Christian imagina-
nation take, which could lead these people into more satisfying
forms of community life, without tainting these forms with a
false idealism? How can the Church, in the manner of its service,
demonstrate that there is hope in Christ, not only for religious
people, but for *the world*? And, finally, how can we manifest it
to those who attempt to hide their hopelessness with religious
illusions, especially when these illusions are Christian, as in
America? Is some attempt, with the aid, say, of Kierkegaard, to
drive men to the boundaries of their existence the only way of
relativising false religion, when its label is Christian, or are we
called, as evangelists, to participate also in this religious revival,
with all its dangers, as the place where a concrete witness to the
Lordship of Christ may be borne?

THE CHURCH

We can summarise the foregoing in four short theses:

1. God is at work in all of world history, calling for decisions

from Christians and non-Christians alike, in the light of his judgment and redemption. This is the overruling reality which sets our basic evangelistic task in East and West.

2. The Church belongs in the world, even at risk to its own structure, alongside of the people in the world, with their concrete problems and questions. Here the Church meets Christ; here the missionary calling becomes concrete, and here, as Christ's body, the Church receives its form.

3. Religion defined as the structure of human attempts to find a foundation or a fulfilment in eternal or absolute truth in their lives, cultures, revolutionary plans is an escape from confrontation with God's will in the crises of this history. Christian faith is never the religious foundation of a culture, but always points to a God who judges and redeems men in relation to their neighbours in the actual world where we are all involved.

4. The Christian's participation in this world is guided by hopeful realism toward it, which upholds a secular realm of relative plans and decisions, relative justice and adjustment of life to life and culture to culture, because he knows the blessing of God on those whose life is service to their neighbour.

What does this mean for our understanding of the form the Church should take in order to share the missionary presence of Christ toward this world? What does it mean for our rethinking of younger and older Churches and mission organisations?

First, must there be a crisis in the relation between the missionary society and the Church which it has founded in order to arrive finally at true partnership in missionary obedience? When Bishop K. H. Ting visited Europe in 1956, he expressed in moving terms his gratitude, that the Church in China, freed from all foreign missionary help and dominance, had at last found itself before God. No less drastic an event than this complete separation could, in his view, have brought the Chinese Church to this maturity and this responsibility. David Paton's contribution to this book has spelled out this necessity in convincing terms.

The case of China is perhaps an extreme one, but mission organisations, as Mr Paton points out, are being asked the same question everywhere. Within the context of historical gratitude for the work which missions have done in planting the seeds of the Gospel throughout the world, has there now come a time in history when they are more of a hindrance than a help to the growing of these seeds? Must the concern of mission-sending Churches learn to find new and different expressions than heretofore? Can a way be found by which financial aid from one Church to another will not bring with it a relation of dominance and dependence? Can the missionary learn to work with and subject to his fellow-Christians in the land to which he is sent, even with regard to questions which touch Christian teaching and Christian witness themselves, so long as he feels himself responsible for the younger Church's theology?

In the conference at Bossey which discussed this problem, it was precisely the younger churchmen, especially from Indonesia, who denied most emphatically that mission-Church relations must go through a crisis, despite the background of Dutch colonialism there. Most of them underlined the point which Mr Sihombing makes, that the first requirement of a missionary is not to be diplomatic but to be brotherly, to get into the church stew along with the people in whose lands he is working. The history of the Churches in Indonesia is very different, however, from that in China or for that matter India or some parts of Africa. The withdrawal of missionary authority over finance and church organisation had already taken place before the war. Nevertheless, a former missionary to Indonesia pointed out that the crisis of relationships is latent in the very fact of the missionary's westernness and difference. The bitter struggle for independence after the war could not help but reflect itself in a nationalism which attacked missionary and foreign connections of the Indonesian Church. The possibility of a crisis in ecumenical or mission relations is inherent in the position of the Church in a society which is rapidly becoming conscious of itself, its strength and its possibilities. There may even come a point where theological correctness is spiritually mistaken. A movement in the churches of East Java during the struggle for independence, for example, took the form of a cultural adaptation which was theologically suspect. Over against this tendency, a confessional group, with the support of missionaries, maintained purity of doctrine, but they did so at the expense of contact with a living culturally creative movement under Christian auspices; and their stand was misinterpreted as dependence, not on the Word of God, but on foreign influence. This is precisely the kind of dilemma in which Chinese Christians have found themselves. They could not maintain doctrinal purity over against Communism until they had been liberated from dependence upon foreign sources for the clarification and expression of this doctrine. Even in the smoothest transition from mission to local Church control, and even in a situation where partnership seems to be a long established fact, the crisis of relations remains latent in the cultural tensions under which we live. There are times when we must be patient, even with heresy, in order to discover the lines along which the Holy Spirit is at work.

How far is the national feeling and the desire for a distinctively national form of Christian life legitimate in any Church, new or old? One study group at Bossey has stated the danger of this most emphatically. 'We are warned, both East and West, that there are dangers in our desire to be indigenous. The Gospel is not western or eastern. It must be shown to be relative to the culture there, but also it stands in judgment on the culture; cultures have been affected by the Gospel, but the understanding of the Gospel has been perverted by nationalist, democratic, Communist and religious systems. Christianity is not individualistic, it is personal and corporate. The Church is a community called apart to save the world, called out to be sent back; the Church is a covenant community.'

The problem poses itself differently, to be sure, in different societies. Mr. Sihombing points out that the problem of adaptation to the culture and society of an independent nation in rapid social change, such as Indonesia, is not to be solved by simple indigenisation. The society has lost its own inner connection with the past through the force of western influence. India, however, would seem to be the country where the cultural forms of a non-Christian society, rooted in centuries of tradition, still exert the most total claim on the moral allegiances of the Christian. The ideals of the unpaid holy-man, of the unorganised religious community, of the intense discipline of mystical meditation, all commend themselves to Christian emulation. In countries, furthermore, where new Churches have become dominant, as in Batakland and Madagascar, the problem of prophetic Christianity over against the cultures of these peoples poses itself in a distinctive way. Remnants of a pre-Christian tradition remain strong in the customs of the people. In Madagascar at least the ability of any foreigner to understand the degree to which these customs can be maintained, and the point at which they must be challenged, has been questioned. Nevertheless, the dominant Christian influence, as in Europe and America, obscures the danger of syncretism on the one side, and poses anew the problem of culture-formation for the Church on the other.

In all this, Christians are called to participate with others in the search for new cultural structures, which will be a combination of that which has been brought in from the West and become a part of the life of Asia and Africa with that in the old culture which has been proved and found adaptable and useful in this new society. The Christian differs fundamentally here from the Mohammedan in being prepared to take over the tradition of his people in pieces, rather than as a religiously moulded whole.

Finally, if the Christian community responds to the will of God which places it in the world, sharing its life, suffering with it, working with that world; thus sharing in Christ's work toward it—what does this mean for the form this Christian community must take in a rapidly changing society? What pattern of the Church is adequate?

This is the question which lies beneath the 'integration' of the International Missionary Council with the World Council of Churches, as it also underlies the controversy that is about to begin about the proper relation of Inter-Church Aid to the other forms of ministry in the world-wide Church. This is the question that underlies the passionate seeking of Christians in China, or in the ashrams of India, or the 'No Church' movement of Japan, for what the Chinese call 'the selfhood of the Church'. This also is the question that prompts some men to 'Industrial Mission' and others to 'House Church' and others again to so radical a rejection of contemporary accepted church forms that they set up 'Pentecostal' assemblies in separation; and many less revolutionary clergy and people are prompted to what are in their own circumstances unprecedented initiatives at the spur of the same insistent enquiry.

This volume is not an answer to this question, because the answer can only be worked out in the practice of Churches around the world, in so-called 'Christendom' and in lands .dominated by non-Christian religions or secular patterns of life. But we can, in concluding, stand for a moment at some of the windows which Hans-Ruedi Weber has opened for us upon this question and look out over the landscape we have yet to explore.[1]

First, how concretely could the ministries of the people of God be so divided and integrated in the Christian community that each supports the whole community in its witness? Mr Weber suggests that the dividing line between office-holders and laymen is becoming fluid. Why indeed should the ministries of teaching, of pastoral counselling and of administration of the sacraments always be united in the same person? What is the relation of the ministry of church organisation and administration to the others? And, on the other hand, how are ministries which involve full-time service of the Church related to the ministries which Christian laymen exercise in their responsibility as members of secular society? How can the profession of business-man, banker or politician become a form of Christian service and witness which not only acts on behalf of the Church in the world but also educates the Church to make its witness as a group in these areas? Frl Cremer has given us an example of two expressions of the Church:

[1] In the work of the Department on the Laity and in its bulletin *Laity*, published twice a year, Mr Weber himself has carried forward many of the insights suggested in his article published here. Interested readers may obtain further information by writing to: Department on the Laity, World Council of Churches, 17 route de Malagnou, Geneva.

the evangelical academies and the YWCA in Germany, exploring and defining a form of ministry, in this case a particular type of Christian social work which is needed among factory women. How can other branches of the Church discover and define such ministries as are needed to meet other needs in modern society? To these questions there is no one single answer but there is a principle to which we are forced and which Mr Weber has enunciated for us: that the Christian community is a community of ministers, just as surely as it is a community of the *laos*—of the laymen, or the people—of God. Within this framework each of us needs to take a fresh look at our function and our place and to discover with our fellow-ministers what the total ministry of the Church is in this world and how it should be divided.

Secondly, what are the *oikoi*—the concrete social groups—in which human beings live today, and how must a Church adjust its structure in order to minister to them there? How should the local congregation, based on a geographical area, interact with other expressions of the Church? Concretely, where may the sacraments be administered, and where not? Where are all the signs of the Church present, and where can we only speak of an *ad hoc* gathering of Christians in the world? Mr Weber has brought home to us that we have lived too long with a mythology of the local congregation, as if it included all classes and groups, whereas actually it generally expresses only the bourgeois or the farming class or one social group over against the others. Few people today would deny the need for Christian groups on the factory floor, in a professional association, or perhaps even in the political party, but opinions divide sharply about the status of these groups. How can one hold them and the local congregation responsible to the whole Church, in which all classes and all interests are represented? Must one perhaps distinguish between the presence of the Church and the fulness of the Church? But then we must ask where the fulness of the Church is to be found. Sociologists tell us that man today lives no longer in one community, where he is one person, but in several different groups in each of which he has different responsibilities and responses. How can the Church become the place where he is united in his responsibility before God? These are the questions to which evangelical academies, projects in industrial evangelism, Christian ashrams in India and house-church movements in various parts of the world, are all experimental responses. They differ significantly from evangelistic movements of the nineteenth century in being consciously responsible to the larger Church even while they challenge it to renew itself in the light of the needs of the world.

In all of this consideration we have not yet faced the question of the unity of the Church as essential to its mission. The reader of this volume will find few direct references to our differing confessional traditions, with their effects on the theology of missions. To a certain extent, this omission is deliberate. We have approached this problem from the point of view of the evangelist in the midst of the world, often at the expense of the perspective of a particular Church. We have tried to take seriously the cry which goes up from every mission field, demanding that we look away from the differences which our separate traditions have created, in order that we may find afresh the missionary calling of our Lord, and the nature of the Church in the light of it. In doing this, to be sure, we discover again that we have differences, and even divisions. The reader will find many of them expressed here and will be able to judge how far they correspond to many of the differences which have been expressed in the Church throughout its history. But the picture of the Church, with its differences, has here been drawn anew, guided by the evangelistic frontiers in Asia, Africa, Europe and America, which enforce upon us at least the discipline of listening to one another in order to discover a common obedience. In the course of this listening we find most acutely that our unity is in many ways still hope and not reality. The chapel of the Ecumenical Institute has not yet become a Church. Ever again we find there that our worship, in which we should experience our greatest togetherness, reveals our disunity most clearly. Even within common traditions we do not find it easy to agree. There is no way out but for the fulness of the various traditions which compose the Ecumenical Movement to be expressed in this chapel. Nevertheless, there is an urgency about our worship, which is a sign of our hope. One cannot participate in the Communion Service of the Church of South India, which so far is that Church with which the largest variety of Christians are in communion, without being confronted with the fact that the conquest of our division is not merely an ideal hope, but a practical necessity for evangelism itself. All of our thinking about the renewal of the Church and the redistribution of its ministries presupposes that Christians come together in one community, in which they can think and pray together, and from which they can go out. This volume is offered as one attempt to discover the outlines of that community.

THE CONTRIBUTORS

DR CHARLES C. WEST (USA) has worked in China and in East Germany and is now Associate Director of the Ecumenical Institute at Bossey, Switzerland. He is author of *Communism and the Theologians.*

FRL MARLIES CREMER (Germany) is Sozialreferentin (Social Work Secretary) with the YWCA and the Evangelical Academy, Bad Boll, Germany.

THE REV. T. SIHOMBING (Indonesia) is a pastor of the Batak Church, and was formerly President of Universitas Nommensen in Sumatra.

THE REV. DAVID M. PATON (Britain), formerly a missionary in China, is Secretary of the Council for Ecumenical Co-operation of the Church Assembly of the Church of England. He is author of *Christian Missions and the Judgment of God*, part author of *Paragraphs for Sundays and Holy Days*, and editor of *Essays in Anglican Self-Criticism.*

DR AREND TH. VAN LEEUWEN (Holland), a missionary of the Dutch Reformed Church formerly in Indonesia and now in Africa, is an expert in Islamic studies.

BISHOP J. E. LESSLIE NEWBIGIN (Britain), Bishop in Madhurai and Ramnad in the Church of South India 1947-59, is now General Secretary of the International Missionary Council. He is author of *The Reunion of the Church*, *The Household of God*, *Sin and Salvation,* and *A South India Diary.*

DR J. BLAUW (Holland) is Secretary of the Dutch Council of Missionary Societies.

THE REV. HANS-RUEDI WEBER (Switzerland), formerly a missionary in Indonesia, is Secretary of the Department on the Laity of the World Council of Churches. He is author of *The Communication of the Gospel to Illiterates.*

304 -17
1-ロ n